Group Work

Theories and Practices

Group Work

Theories and Practices

H.Y. Siddiqui

RAWAT PUBLICATIONS
Jaipur • New Delhi • Bangalore • Guwahati • Kolkata

ISBN 978-81-316-0171-6 (hardback)

Reprinted, 2022

Published by
Prem Rawat for **Rawat Publications**
Satyam Apts, Sector 3, Jawahar Nagar, Jaipur 302 004 (India)
Phones: 0141 265 1748 / 265 7006
E-mail: info@rawatbooks.com
Website: www.rawatbooks.com

New Delhi Office
4858/24, Ansari Road, Daryaganj, New Delhi 110 002
Phone: 011 2326 3290

Also at Bangalore, Guwahati and *Kolkata*

Typeset by Rawat Computers, Jaipur
Printed at Nice Printing Press, New Delhi

This book is dedicated to the memory of

Mr. & Mrs. M.Y. Siddiqui,
my parents, who invested in me.

Mr. John B. Collins,
a friend, who I could not meet, from Ardfert, Kerry, Ireland, who being a "Pioneer" never touched a drop of alcohol in his life.

My brothers *Hasan Yasin Siddiqui and Sibtain Yasin Siddiqui,*
who died young, yet contributed a great deal to my life.

Contents

Acknowledgements

I am indebted to a number of people in writing this text, but it is difficult to mention them all individually. Professor Doreen Elliott at Arlington, Texas helped me in acquiring the required material, by introducing me to Mr. Donald Capps, the Web and Technology Specialist, who helped me in locating the articles on the internet. Professor Nazneen, from Arlington, Texas had agreed to write an introduction to the text, but could not to do it for health reasons. Yet, her involvement encouraged me to review many things. Bruce and Mary Jane from Colorado, and Angie and Randy Herman from Minnesota kept faith in my ability to do the job. I thank my colleagues and students in the Department of Social Work in Mizoram University for encouraging me to complete the task. Mr. Arif Haider worked hard on the formatting of the manuscript. My thanks to Rawat Publications for agreeing to publish the text.

Farida, Eraj, Yukie, my daughter-in-law, Standy Collins, my son-in-law and Seema, provided the much needed moral support. I am grateful to all of them.

H.Y. Siddiqui

Preface

The use of groups in developing countries like India, is somewhat different than that in the West, as is the case with other methods. Group work for a variety of reasons, has not been very popular in social work practice in India, though it has been a part of the social work curriculum since the beginning of social work education in India. In practice, however, the social workers have not made full use of the potential of the method. Social work practice in the beginning was mainly rooted in psychological problems of individuals and case work was the preferred approach. Potential of the group and its influence on individual values and behaviour was not well acknowledged in the early forties, as the research on groups was at a very nascent stage of its development and has still not made much progress in developing countries.

Social work practice overall, has not been able to demonstrate either then or now, the potential of group work in India. As a result the method did not get the attention it deserved. The art of using a group for designing "helping interventions" is still not fully developed. It is therefore, neither adequately learned nor used in actual practice. A simple reason for its relegation to a secondary status in India is the continuing emphasis in social work practice on casework and on community work. Social work practice is still largely conceived as helping individuals facing problems of social functioning, or interventions designed to work with communities, both urban and rural, to promote development. Since the main focus is either the individual or a community, the work is seen as casework or community work.

Another problem which leads to its stagnation, is the lack of literature on group work dealing with indigenous situations such as self-help groups in rural areas. Examples of working with clients, who have to be motivated to join a group, are missing in the literature produced in the West. Group work in developed countries addresses a very different set of clients and the problems faced by them. The clients' "needs" and "motivations to join a group" are different, which makes it difficult for an Indian student to realize the potential of the method here. My motivation for writing the text is to help the students understand the local context and still use the insights and theories of group work developed globally. Further, the rising cost of foreign texts is making it difficult for many schools to acquire these for the students in sufficient numbers.

The first chapter provides an introduction to group work practice in India, looking at the local clients and their needs. The second and third chapters deal with the social science findings on groups and various theories developed globally to explain different facets of functioning of groups. The fourth chapter provides a discussion of group processes signifying the major events in a group, while the fifth chapter deals with principles of working with a group in a historical perspective, to provide the reader an idea of the thinking that went into conceptualizing these principles. It also provides a rationale of how we should formulate these in our own context. The sixth chapter deals with the process of working with a group, giving a detailed account of the different stages involved. The chapter provides specific guidelines of activities, such as planning, consolidating, evaluation and termination in the Indian context. The seventh chapter highlights the skills needed and the eighth chapter looks at techniques to be used in working with a group.

The text then focuses on the practice of group work in working with children, youth and elderly in the ninth chapter, with women in the tenth chapter, and concludes with a chapter on self-help groups, highlighting the uses in India, Bangladesh, Pakistan and Sri Lanka. I hope that the text will be helpful to students in developing countries and they would be able to use the method with greater understanding with different clients.

H.Y. Siddiqui

1

Introduction to Group Work

Social work as a profession emerged to provide a variety of services to individuals, groups and communities in the developing countries. The improvement in the social functioning of the individuals was a major objective. Group is a very natural response of humans as they love interacting with others. They come together in groups to achieve a number of needs which can only be met through collective efforts. Human groups as such constitute an important social unit in all societies. Social functioning competence depends to a great extent on the experiences of persons in their interactions with people in their social environment. Cooley (1909) was one of the earliest group theorists to highlight the importance of group experience and to point out that it was by group experience that the individual becomes socialized. Socialization results in social learning. Social learning implies that the individual learns about values, norms, acceptable behaviour, and life style through interaction with others. This process seems to be most influenced by small groups such as family, friends, peer groups in school, play groups, occupational and neighbourhood groups and so on.

It is, therefore, imperative for social work as a helping profession dealing with social functioning issues and competence to understand groups and their functioning and impact on members. The idea that group can be used as a medium to help did not originate within social work profession, though working with groups was accepted as a part of social work interventions in USA, where the activity first emerged as a helping activity. Working with group as a method of helping people emerged as an independent professional activity and only later merged with the social work profession. Since then it was incorporated as a method of social work in the USA. There are mixed reactions among those who were associated with its growth since its inception about how the merger with social work has affected its development and its current status as a social work method in USA. As Andrews suggests, group work's identification with social work was motivated by a desire to professionalize and to find a place in the university. After interviewing a number of early practitioners, she concluded that according to some this merger blunted the radical spirit of group work (see Jains, 2001). Klein (1972) suggests that the numerical strength of group workers was small compared to case workers in the US; they, influenced by the clinical approach of these workers, diluted their own emphasis in group work practice on social action and prevention. Glasser and Mayadas (1986) were more emphatic when they concluded that the merger of group work with social work was the death knell of group work as a unique methodology. In USA the group work's focus thus gradually shifted to individuals instead of being on group and its potential (Middleman, 1981). This is still the case in social work practice in general in the West, where individual problems, in particular mental health issues, predominate the practice. Group work is no exception. Group work, however, is an accepted method of intervention though its focus may still be on individual needs and problems. But this should not lead one to think that this is the only objective which group work as a method can be used to achieve.

The use of groups in developing countries like India has been somewhat different than that of the West. Yet, as is the case in USA but perhaps for a very different set of reasons, it has not been very popular in social work education and practice. Group work has been a part of social work curriculum since the beginning of social work education in India. In practice, however, the social workers have not made full use of the potentials of the method. Social workers working with children, youth and women either in government organizations such as children's institutions, prisons, and family welfare organizations, or in non governmental organizations where social workers usually found employment, focused more on individual and community problems. Social work practice in the beginning was mainly rooted in psychological problems of individuals and the case work was the preferred approach. The potential of group and its influence on individual values and behaviour was not well acknowledged even in the early forties as the research on groups was in a very nascent stage of its development. Even now it has not made much progress in the developing countries. Social work has not been able to demonstrate either then or now the potential of group work practice in India. As a result, the method did not get the attention it deserved. The art of using the group for designing helping interventions is still not fully developed. It is neither adequately learned nor used in actual practice. A simple reason for its relegation to a secondary status in India is the continuing emphasis of social work practice on casework and on community work. Social work practice in India is still largely conceived as interventions in the lives of individuals facing problems of different kinds, or on interventions designed to work with communities, either urban or rural in character, in order to promote their development or organization. Since the main focus is either individual or community the work is seen as casework or community work. However, in both cases, the worker has to work with groups as well, but that is not seen as the main objective or method of intervention. Ironically when the worker is working with a group such as family it is not seen as group work practice either. Such interventions are generally termed as family social work or social work with families. Family is seen as a natural group and group work in social work is generally seen as a process of working with purposely designed and structured groups. This focus of social work practice on individuals or communities leads to development of positions such as case workers and community workers in different organizations. This has helped in popularizing the idea that social workers are either case workers or community workers. In fact in many schools of social work now the major focus of the field practicum is on case work and community work in the curriculum. The group work thus gets relegated to a sort of secondary method.

In 1936 the American Association for the Study of Group Work was founded and in the same year social work education began in India. Indian society was undergoing the same kind of problems, such as migrants converging in major cities in India in large numbers and living in slum conditions. These conditions led many socially conscious groups to work with them to mitigate their sufferings. Many activities were conducted in groups such as attempts to organize workers to demand better working conditions and facilities, informal education activities, recreational activities, health and hygiene related activities, etc. That these activities could strengthen the democratic behaviour among members was however not anticipated. The emphasis remained on community welfare and individual counselling activities. When the need for trained workers to carry out these activities was felt, social work education was conceptualized. Group work was seen as an integral part but social work right from the beginning put greater emphasis on an understanding of individual personality to motivate people in general to change their conditions, and to a lesser extent, an environment modification amounting to service delivery. So the focus on group work as a method was not very pronounced in teaching, as perhaps what the method could deliver was not very clear in the minds of either the educators or the practitioners.

In India the concept of group work practice was largely influenced by the work of Trecker (1948), Wilson and Ryland (1949), *Konopka* (1963) etc. As is the case with other methods of social work in India, not much has been written on the subject, inviting criticism of over reliance on American texts. In a review article on group work literature in India, Joseph (1997) brings out the dismal picture. Group work according to Trecker (1948) is a process through which individuals in groups are helped to acquire experiences of relating with others. The group itself is seen as a source of help to individuals. This notion of using group leads to its purposeful construction and the group work practice gets identified with the idea of formation of group and subsequently working with it to help to achieve different objectives or goals. For a number of years group work as an activity was conceived in the recreation setting as organizing groups of children and youths largely for engaging them during their leisure time with the added responsibility of sorting out their relationship problems within the play groups or modifying their anti social behaviours such as using abusive language, smoking, etc. A usual query to test the understanding of the students was to ask them to explain the difference between the role of a physical instructor and a social worker. Group work practice was not seen as related to solving individual problems like poverty. The discovery of group as a link to empowerment, providing support, meeting economic needs through income generation, etc. is a very recent phenomenon.

Group work practice in India and other developing countries makes very little use of group process for therapeutic purposes. Very few social workers have used group as a medium to help clients in the psychiatric setting. Social workers working with families also are relying more on individual counselling rather than using the group process. The objective of group work practice in general is to use group process for task orientation such as capacity building, enabling members to acquire information, learning to participate in decision-making within a group, and learning to carry out group tasks of different kinds. The rule of democracy to meet your own needs and help others to meet their needs is supposed to be the underlying philosophy. The democratic objectives and ethics of equal opportunities are more generally pursued in children's and adolescent's groups, in India. The activity focus is generally on recreation and meeting socio-emotional needs of individual members and carrying out socially useful and productive activities as well. These objectives thus would fall more in the growth oriented group work category. A more recent use of group work is to form common interest groups or self-help groups to help specific clients for achieving specific needs through collective efforts. Formation of self-help groups is a major activity thrust in working with poor women in particular, with the objective of promoting income generation or saving and credit groups. This activity thrust is more in the arena of task oriented group work.

Use of groups has become popular in community work practice as well in the recent emphasis on development. In India various community workers are forming various kinds of groups for meeting community needs or delivery of services in the community. The thrust of these groups is not to use the group process or interaction among members to facilitate the growth of individual members but is more on achievement of group tasks. A similar use of group is made in achieving organizational objectives. Many industrial and commercial organizations are using groups for reviewing their processes for task achievement, increasing productivity, improving in plant relationships and for promoting employee welfare as well.

An important characteristic of group work in India is that groups are formed with a long-term perspective to become self-sufficient and to get institutionalized. It could be debated whether all of this is group work or only the former. The argument in this book is that the scope of group work has expanded in recent years and that intending students can use the expansion in scope and development in knowledge about groups in various disciplines, to work with different kinds of client groups. The skills of working with the groups are developed and used in the wider context of overall expertise of human relations developed by social work profession, using the theoretical insights developed by social sciences and the experience gained by social work practitioners and other helping professions.

The Use of Groups in Social Work

Within social work practice, groups are effectively used to support individuals in growth, rehabilitation, personal change, and for prevention of social and personal breakdown. A group can also be used for the development and change of the group's own environment, for modifying systems, and for changing some of the institutions of society. A recent study (see Mayadas et al. 2004) of global trends in group work, however found that the curriculum in most schools of social work globally emphasized individual needs such as support, therapy and self development, as the focus of group work practice. Only in South America social change was seen as an objective of group work. While experience in social work practice has produced evidence that certain ends can be achieved through practice with groups, there has been relatively little research to establish empirically the outcome of group interventions. In India, only now such efforts are beginning to take place. In particular the impact of self-help groups has been studied by several researchers. Groups have been used in developing countries when they somehow seemed to be the appropriate means of service delivery for social development, meeting economic needs, preparation for new experiences, education, recreation, changing values, modification of lifestyle, providing support, problem solving, community planning, and many other purposes. It may not be wrong to suggest that group work has been used in many developing countries as a supplementary intervention for achieving the broad goals of community organization or social development.

Social science research on groups, however, has produced enough evidence on the effects of groups in influencing individual attitudes and values, and achieving goals, but not so in influencing or changing the system or societal situation outside of the group. However, it is possible to use groups for a variety of objectives with different client groups. Hartford (1972) has suggested three broad categories of use of group interventions:

1. Where the focus is on members: socialization-re-socialization, acquiring or changing concept of self, identity, motivation; attitude formation and change, formation and modification of values and beliefs; behavioural change; achieving a sense of belonging and support; education;
2. Where the focus is task orientation: economic activities, social tasks or awareness generation, particularly about group, community or social situation.
3. For change in social situation or conditions outside the group: (a) modification of the institution or social system within which the group exists, or (b) of the social situation – including the community or society – through pressure, dissemination of information, or organization; modification of attitudes of outsiders.

Hartford therefore considers the scope of group work ranging from influencing individuals to accomplishing social change. This is what is being practiced in the developing countries. As we shall see, social workers have used the medium of group for accomplishing a variety of objectives. The definition of group work in developing countries thus has to be recast to include this vast scope of group use.

Definitions of Group Work

In order to evolve a clear understanding of what group work is, and the changes it has undergone since its inception, it will be useful to scan the definitions given by different authors. Marjorie Murphy (1959) for example defined social group work as "enhancement of person's social functioning through purposeful group experiences." Murphy is simply focusing on the potential of group experiences and the way these can be used to help individuals to grow. In other words the group work helps individuals to acquire more effective ways of dealing with their own feelings and behaviour within the group. It is interesting to note, as Konopka (1963) pointed out, that this definition is very similar to the one Perlman has for casework. Perlman (1957) defined casework as "a process to help individuals to cope more effectively with their problems in social functioning." This indicates the similarity of scope in casework and group work, i.e., to keep the focus on individual rather than on the collective goals or objectives. Trecker (1948) arrived at his definition of social group work by focusing on interaction in the group as well. According to him, "the group worker enables various types of groups to function in such a way that both group interaction and programme activities contribute to the growth of individual and the achievement of desirable social goals." Trecker has thus expanded the scope of group work to add the achievement of group goals, apart from individual need fulfillment. As many authors noted that recreation and democracy were the two movements, which have influenced early conceptualization of group work in addition to the idea of self-help (see Konopka, 1963). As Mary Parker Follett (1934), the noted political scientist, observed, "we do not get the whole power of the group unless every individual is given full value, and is giving full values." The initial concept of group work therefore was largely working with the objectives of providing members equal opportunities for participation in group activities and to meet their needs, and at the same time, to fulfil some broader concerns of democracy as well. The group work thus began as a method for capacity building or as an enabling process rather than a problem solving method or process.

Sallie Bright (1955), however, felt that group work can address the two-fold objectives of providing therapeutic services as also the political goal of strengthening democratic functioning, a sentiment which is repeated by Balgopal and Vassili in 1983. They emphasize the environment-group and individual relationship. They felt that, "the general goals of group work include both improving normal functioning and neutralizing the abnormal functioning of individuals." Skidmore (1988) used a similar approach by identifying group work purposes as "reducing or eliminating roadblocks to social interaction and accomplishing desirable social goals". In 1980 it was felt in the US that many professions were using group work as a method of practice, such as nurses, psychologists, counsellors, psychiatrists, teachers, clergy and many others. They employ treatment group methods while managers, supervisors, politicians and community organizers use task group methods, yet there is hardly any conceptual agreement or clarity regarding its definition, purpose, practice methods and technique (Toseland and Rivas, 2001). However, the authors defined group work as "goal directed activity with small groups of people aimed at meeting socio-emotional needs and accomplishing tasks. The activity is directed at individual members of a group and to the group as a whole within a system of social service delivery." This obviously is a very different perspective of group work. In this perspective the main purpose is to master the art of handling a group situation. The group is expected to meet socio-emotional needs of individuals and accomplish group tasks. In self-help groups for example, which have become very popular now, the task of the groups are to function in such a way that members can benefit from them in a variety of ways. The emphasis is however not on providing equal benefits or equal powers to all. It was so right from the beginning and every one was provided an equal opportunity but not an equal share. However, a group has the right to frame its own rules and develop its own norms and culture. The task objectives coming to acquire more prominence, became a new thrust in group work practice. It also extended the scope of group work practice beyond the scope of professional social work, opening it for many other professions. As Konopka (1963) pointed out, the history of the development of modern group work is part of the history of social agencies evolving within a changing society. The older social services distinguished sharply between the giver and the receiver, and therefore the new services thought of the concept of self-help. It was mainly to emphasize the value of hard work and rejecting charity as a principle to solve problems. As a political objective it also implied collective power to handle common problems and as such signified a shift from seeking patronage from powerful elites. In more recent times it signifies reducing dependence on state. In clinical terms also group counselling began with the objective of saving time by dealing collectively with clients and only later the potential of group to contribute significantly to achieve therapeutic goals was realized, and thus the concept of self-help received further support. In clinical term the terms self-help refers to members attempting to resolve their problems without the help or intervention of professionals.

In the Indian context group work will refer to working with a small group (members ranging from 7 to 10) to a medium size group (members ranging from 10 to 20) for a variety of purposes beginning from recreation to behaviour modification on the one hand, and accomplishing tasks including social change and development on the other, with a variety of clients ranging from children to elderly. The worker makes use of the expertise in human relationships to help these groups to achieve the group goals in a participatory manner while paying adequate attention to individual needs and social norms.

Group counselling is similar to group work but it requires a more specific clinical orientation. Group counselling is used for both therapeutic and educational purposes and also for a combination of the two.

Similarly, group counselling has both preventive as well as remedial objectives. It uses an interpersonal process that analyses thoughts, feelings and behaviour, and the emphasis is on discovering the internal sources of strengths. Common techniques include reflection, interpretation, clarification and role-playing. Ideally, the members decide for themselves the specific goals of the group. The group offers understanding and support. The group provides a sample of reality experienced by the members, whose struggles and conflicts are similar to those experienced by them outside the group. The diverse nature of members provides them an opportunity to see themselves through the eyes of others in a safe environment. This feedback is a major source for them to rethink their coping approaches. Group therapy or group psychotherapy is a process of reeducation of both conscious and unconscious awareness including both the present and the past. The goal is a major or minor transformation of personality structure. This requires a more specialised knowledge on the part of the professional. The therapist generally helps to recreate the past for individual members and facilitates them to cope with it by using the support and understanding in the group to affect new strategies for meeting these in future. The experience also helps in reducing the pent up tensions and anxieties.

Current Use of Groups in India

Group Work with Children and Youth

Group work with children and youth is one of the earliest uses of group work in India. In many organizations working with children social workers organize groups to work with both children and youths with a variety of objectives such as:

Recreational Groups: Recreational groups are fairly common where the idea is to engage children in their leisure time to organize outdoor games. Though the major objective is providing recreational activities but the worker helps the group to evolve norms for decision-making and encourages wider participation of members in decision-making, developing a sense of fair play, respecting minority opinions and inculcating an understanding of diversity.

Educational Groups: In educational groups the main focus of the group activities is to pursue some educational objectives. Informal education through groups, helping slow learners, mainstreaming out of school children and youth, and dealing with problems of drop out, are some popular uses of group for educational purposes. Use of groups in educational camps is also commonly found in India. Helping youth to acquire value education and skills to become self-employed, and generating awareness about drug use, HIV/AIDS, and other health related issues through the process of group formation, are popular activities.

Support Groups: Support groups for children and youth are generally formed to discuss problems being faced by them and to look for solutions. Street children, working children, children and youth having drug related problems, orphan children, children and youth facing trauma and so on, are helped through support group activities. A major focus in support groups, as stated earlier, is to provide a forum where these children and youths can come together, either alone or with relevant experts, to discuss the common problems being faced by them and look for ways to cope with these in more personally satisfying and socially acceptable ways. Working with adolescent girls facing violence or abuse through support group has been found to be quite effective.

Remedial Groups: Remedial groups are meant to use group interaction and programme activities to modify behavioural responses of members. School social workers, probation officers and social workers working in children's home, observation homes and other organizations dealing with delinquent children and youth coming in conflict with law, have used groups for remedial activities. The main objective of these groups is to help children and adolescents to review their present situation, learn new coping strategies to adjust with the new environment and start thinking about the future. This is an area of group work practice which has not adequately developed and practitioners face problems as few are equipped to deal adequately with the challenge and no mechanism of supervision exists.

Group Work with Women

Working with groups of women has become very popular in recent times and a lot of organizations working with women are forming groups of women for a variety of objectives. Self-help groups of women have become very effective to accomplish a wide variety of objectives. These groups address such goals as:

Education: Providing education to women on different aspects concerning their life beginning from literacy skills to legal, social and political issues through the use of group work activities is emerging as a major area of work in many organizations. Women of all ages and of all kinds belonging to both rural and urban areas and different socio-economic groups, castes and religions are participating in such groups. However the main focus is deprived groups, both in rural or urban areas. The main objectives are providing information and awareness leading to better handling of their present day situations at work and at home. These groups may or may not consider advocating or mobilizing women for social change. Education and awareness building is the major goal irrespective of what it delivers.

Support: Support groups are being used to work with women facing domestic violence and abuse both at home and work places by a variety of professionals in India. Such groups, besides providing a forum for women to share their experiences and receive emotional support, have also considered making women active in developing networks and using advocacy and social action to prevent violence against women. Support groups of women sex workers and women suffering from HIV/AIDS are also being formed to help such women in India.

Livelihood: One of the most common objectives of forming groups of women is to provide them economic help. A number of self-help groups are being organized for helping them to learn to save and to create a fund as a source for getting financial help from a more friendly and non-exploitative source for their day to day need. Women are also being helped to acquire economic skills of different kinds to augment their incomes by starting, either individually or collectively, small business enterprises. The group is used as a mechanism to link them with financial institutions and government agencies in order to encourage them to participate in developmental activities. It is expected to enhance their access to resources and to develop cooperative attitudes in their struggle against poverty and exploitation.

Legal Aid: Some organizations are using groups to work with women to provide them legal aid concerning marital problems, inheritance matters, sexual harassment and many other aspects concerning their lives. Group is used as a facilitative mechanism for imparting legal help as women find it difficult to individually contemplate any legal initiative to deal with their problems.

Health Groups: Use of group for providing health related information to expecting mothers, mothers with newly born babies or women suffering from various ailments is also being used by a variety of professionals in India. Besides providing information the groups are also being used for inducing behavioural changes or attitudinal changes among women.

Group Work with Elderly

Group activities with elderly are also being undertaken by many organizations working with them.

Support Group: Support groups for elderly persons are helpful in dealing with the feeling of depression, a problem considered normal in old age. Loss of active life, reduction in income, power and physical health, induces a sense of loneliness and hence a feeling of depression. Support groups help in overcoming these feelings, and sharing of individual accounts in groups help to reduce the feeling of loneliness and the accompanying anxiety.

Recreational Groups: In day care centres of elderly people recreation groups are formed to organize recreational activities. These groups also become support groups at times.

Health Groups: Some professionals are using groups to provide information and to bring attitudinal changes relating to health among the elderly in India as well.

Group Work with Workers

Work Groups: Groups are being organized at work places by social workers and other professionals to provide a variety of services to employees.

Legal Aid: Many professionals in India are providing legal aid to workers to raise their awareness about their rights and also help them to engage in collective bargaining through the use of groups.

Improving Productivity: Use of small groups in India in work places to improve productivity is also being done by inducing quality circles and the concept of team building.

Welfare Services: Some organizations have formed groups of employees to manage canteens, transport and housing services. Formation of cooperative societies is also a popular group activity.

Group Work with Communities

Groups have been used for promoting community organization and development goals in both urban slums and rural areas. The workers working with the community find it more pragmatic to divide the community in to smaller groups either based on clients such as women, youth, farmers and so on, or geographic segments such as lane or a particular ward in a larger urban neighbourhood (see Siddiqui, 1997). The general purpose of these groups is to discuss problems faced by the community or a section of the community and to try to redress them. The overall goals thus address the community needs although the needs of the group members are also addressed in the process. In some cases such groups may also address social issues within the community such as status of women, caste relationships or issues relating to child labour and child abuse. The groups within a community may also come together to form an umbrella organization at the community level. In some cases they may assume a wider role which may even extend beyond the community goals. Many women's related community groups have assumed greater social significance in some areas.

Computer-Based Group Work

Computer-based group work practice has not emerged in India as yet as one does not find any mention of it in the syllabus of schools of social work in India. There are a few reported uses of computer groups from practice in the social work literature (Abell and Galinsky, 2002) in the United States of America. Group workers, both practitioners and educators, are not very comfortable with such groups (Galinsky, Schopler and Abell, 1997). At the present juncture in India social work practice is preoccupied with poor and deprived populations generally, hence the possibility of computer-based group work practice appears rather remote. Yet, as we suggest later in the text, a professional should be willing to offer services to all, both the poor and the rich, and the scope of practice may expand in future. There is no harm in learning how to incorporate modern technology in group work practice. In computer-based groups the clients do not have to travel to the meeting place and may or may not meet other members face to face. Group sites can be created and accessed now through use of internet. Those clients in particular, who may either not have time or are unable to travel can be the prime beneficiaries of computer-based group work practice.

Computer groups can be used for support and providing information to otherwise inaccessible populations. In India some clients may prefer anonymity to discuss personal problems. Both discussion groups where you can post your message any time and online chat rooms where communication is more quick can be used.

Future of Group Work in India

The focus of group work practice is not clinical in nature as we suggested earlier and I do not anticipate that in future the treatment concerns will dominate group work practice. It is ironic that group work practice in United States, where social work practice is far more professional in nature, seems to be declining and facing a rather bleak future, as some leading group workers seem to suggest (Kurland et al., 2004). What is more important is that the students feel that the meaning of group work and what a group worker can do is not very clear. Further there seem to be little importance given to what the group workers do since it has very little to do with therapeutic work (Kelsey, 2003, as quoted in Kurland et al., 2004). This should be an eye opener for group work educators everywhere. If the group work practice in particular and social work practice in general has to become more effective the curriculum inputs and teaching methodology both have to be updated and made more scientific in nature. The future of group work is very bright in India as the popularity of self-help groups not only in India but in many developing countries, indicate. Group work is already beginning to emerge as the central strategy in development programmes in many developing countries.

Till date no association of group workers has ever been formed in India, nor is one needed perhaps. However, it is unfortunate that no serious effort for the study of working with groups has been done in India. The method specialization was never used in India; instead a field-based specialization emerged. Social workers in a medical setting are called medical social workers, those working in mental hospitals as psychiatric social workers and those working in prisons as probation officers or social workers in the correctional setting and so on. There are some positions of case workers and community workers in India but hardly any of group workers even now. The current situation notwithstanding, all social workers can learn and use group work to facilitate their work with their clients.

2

Social Science Research on Groups

Small Group Research

The small group research remains inconclusive despite the fact that several attempts have been made and are still being made to study what happens in a small group when people come together for a variety of purposes and interact with each other for a considerable duration (see Levine and Moreland, 1990). Two approaches to study small groups can readily be identified. One is through the use of laboratories where experimental designs have been used to study the dynamics of small groups. The other is the field method where anthropologists and social workers have observed the groups in actual day to day happenings. If the laboratories have produced what could be termed as 'scientific understanding', then the findings should be collaborated by the field experiences, but that consistency has not yet been demonstrated (Kivisto, 2003: 298). There are still many questions such as, is cohesiveness good or bad for a group. The general belief among social workers is that it is the ultimate that a group worker strives for. Yet recent studies on cohesiveness in groups are questioning its impact on performance of the group (see Langfred, 1998; Barbara et al., 1998). There is still no unanimity about what changes take place in the temporal environment of a group and why. In other words, our knowledge about group development is far from adequate; as Levine and Moreland (1990) pointed out, the results of the studies on group development are difficult to evaluate, as they involve qualitative analyses of a few groups (often only one). These studies are not always clear about such issues as the number of stages through which groups develop, the behaviours exhibited by group members during those stages, the rate at which group development occurs, and so on. Most theorists argue that group development is a recapitulation of the childhood experiences of individual group members. Other factors that might affect group development, such as (a) the beliefs and expectations that current members share about their group (Long 1984); (b) the entry of new members or the departure of old ones (Moreland and Levine 1988; Arrow and Mcgrath, 1993); and (c) changes in the group's physical or social environment (Gersick, 1988), are rarely acknowledged. Arrow et al. (2004) in their study of temporal environment in groups reported that the temporal perspective is a process focused view that treats groups as systems in which changes occur across multiple time scales. Two of the themes in the literature identified by the authors who reviewed the literature that takes a temporal perspective on groups are: (a) group processes have temporal patterns; and (b) groups are complex systems characterized by nonlinear dynamics. The authors therefore concluded that there is a need for more research and theory development as nothing conclusive is there. Similarly Vecchio et al. (2006), in their study of the utility of situational leadership theory pointed out that they agreed with earlier studies that the theory has little practical utility. Similar sentiments were expressed by Forte (1994) who specifically did a content analysis of literature on group work published by authors from four countries in the form of journal articles. He concluded that studies were not research based but were descriptions of practice with only elementary data analysis. According to him the literature as such made little contribution to the knowledge base of group work.

Yet, the research studies have come up with some assumptions and trends which can help the group workers in understanding the individual behaviour in a group. They have highlighted the group functioning and how interaction in groups unleashes a number of processes that influence the behaviour of individual members and the achievement of group goals. Some of these ideas have been listed below for helping those planning to work with groups.

Group activity is a normal part of all living beings including small insects. It is common to see ants working in groups to carry food or to see birds flying in groups. The need for groups arises as many activities are only possible through group efforts. A human being spends a great part of the time living in groups. It is therefore natural for any service profession to understand groups and their importance, possible uses and their dynamics. Social science experts have devoted a great deal of time in studying groups. Yet, as is the case with many other topics, there is little unanimity about the conclusions drawn about groups and their functioning and possible impact on human behaviour. The discussion of studies here is not exhaustive; only those studies which highlight a particular aspect of group functioning have been referred to. We have tried to summarize efforts to study various aspects of groups such as its definition, its impact on members, and possibility of its use as a medium to effect changes in groups, communities and even society in general. In India the efforts to study groups have been rather scant, hence generally we have to rely on studies done elsewhere. An attempt has however been made to refer to studies more relevant to social work practice with groups in developing countries.

Definitions of Group

Many attempts have been made to define a group, but as we can see the differences in defining the same persist. Eubank formulated a definition of group in 1932, as follows:

> "[a group is] two or more individuals in a relationship of psychic interaction, whose relationship with one another may be abstracted and distinguished from their relationship with all others so that they may be thought of as an entity."

Karl Mannheim (1957), while talking of groups also in 1932, however, felt that groups consisting of two or three persons are quasi groups and do not need group norms and that they represent purely personal relationships. It is obvious that when we are considering a group as a social formation, certain basic characteristics such as structure, norms and functions are what we expect to find in it. Considering this, some scholars have argued that a group as a cohesive entity can only be found among adolescents, as children up to age 9 form groups which are more in the nature of agglomeration of inter-linked dyads whose composition change frequently (Grusec and Lytton, 1988). Mills (1967) defined group as, "a set of single organisms, commonly called members, which over a period of time or multiple interrupted periods, relate to each other face to face, processing matter-energy and information."

Giddens (1989) noted that social group is "a number of people who interact with each other on a regular basis." It is different from aggregate, a collection of people in the same place and same time but having no definite connection with each other, and social category, a statistical grouping that is people classified together on the basis of any characteristic. Lang (1981, 1986) talks of three terms, i.e., aggregate, collectivity and group, while trying to define a group. To him aggregate of persons refers to persons coming together temporarily for any reason or purpose while a collectivity is a plurality of persons having a social structure, collective consciousness and interaction between themselves. A group on the other hand has a common identity, a feeling of unity and shared goals and norms. Lang sees these as a continuum and a process. Collectivity and group have a lot of overlap and it will be difficult to distinguish traits which are not common. Collective consciousness may be found in people spread across the world and the term collective is generally used to describe a large and abstract category which exercises considerable influence on individual members. In the communist social structure a collective is a small group formed to replace the family. A more pragmatic definition of the group is, two or more persons who come together to achieve any objective. Karl Manheim (1957) differentiated between the groups which had two, three or four members and called them quasi groups, as we pointed out earlier. He called group of two members a couple and said that members of a couple have a more permanent influence on each other. Another important insight he offered was that the less individualized the members of a couple are, the easier is its functioning. He further said that groups of two or three persons do not need group norms as they represent a personal relationship. The larger the group the greater is the need to have uniformity of thought and attitude for the functioning of the group. Manheim was looking at the group as a social force trying to integrate individuals. The main characteristics of groups that he identified are:

A relative organization meaning some kind of division of roles and functions among members; group norms, ideas about existence or purpose of group and its relationship with other groups; collective interest and individual interest; and a system of distributing power; and repressions and conflicts and mechanisms to deal with these.

Manheim was able to visualize the entire process of group development from its stage of inception to functioning stage when he talked of role differentiation, emergence of group norms and goals. He was also aware of the problems the group was likely to encounter in its functioning, which were those of individual interests and conflicts associated with power distribution. Therefore there was need for mechanisms to deal with these issues in order to restore order in group functioning. He however did not use the word group process or development, nor did he offer any explanation to analyze group dynamics. His major interest was how a group formation can integrate individuals, which still continues to be one of the concerns among professionals working with groups. He discovered these insights in 1932 and went on to explain some other aspects of functioning of groups in more details in his lectures, which were later published under the title *Systematic Sociology* in 1957.

Classification of Groups

Cooley (1909) used the term 'primary group' to refer to a small association of people connected by ties of an emotionally involving nature. A 'secondary group' on the other hand consists of a number of people who meet regularly but who do not have intimate ties with each other. Some people consider a group secondary where people do not come face to face with each other despite belonging to a group. According to some, the distinction between the two types of groups is not very clear.

Groups are classified by Tonnies (1955) into communities and association. By community he meant any circle of people who live together and share a whole set of interests. He saw groups as the tribe, the village, the city and the nation, and association as a group organized for a specific interest or a group of interests in common.

Some other types of groups are 'formal' and 'informal' groups. A formal group is created by already existing rules such as a formal department in an organization, a committee or a commission formed for carrying out a specific task, etc., while an informal group is a peer group of children in a slum or school. The former can also be called a task group, although an informal group can also become a task group once it decides to carry out a specific task such as raising the awareness level of the community regarding some problem or the other. This example shows that it is not useful to give labels to groups as they may fall under different categories at the same time. To understand a group we may have to look at its features or characteristics, and not what category it belongs to. However, in order to become familiar with different terms used to describe the groups we are giving some terms which are in common usage, such as common interest groups, self-help groups, command group, therapeutic groups, peer group and so on. These terms signify the nature or the purpose of the group.

Common interest group is a term used to describe people having some special needs, who come together to form a group to meet these needs, for example small farmers in a village coming together to resolve their water resource shortages, or acquiring new technology, seeds or fertilizer. In an urban setting a group may be one of small entrepreneurs coming together to resolve their financial problems or acquiring new technology or developing a marketing strategy, etc.

Self-help groups are similarly formed to meet any specific need or a group of needs through collective efforts. Currently self-help group is a term popularly in use to describe groups of people particularly women, generally poor women, who come together to form a group to meet various needs. The general idea behind promoting self-help groups is to reduce the dependence of the common people on outside agencies. The self-help group movement also aims at developing a meaningful partnership between micro and macro systems. Self-help groups in India and Bangladesh, where the idea of self-help group to meet economic needs were successfully used, use self-help groups to provide the common man access to credit from macro financial institutions. We shall look at the working of these groups in more detail later. Self-help group in developed countries, however, refer to a group of people, who come together to seek solutions to their problems without any direct intervention from professional helpers, although the professional helpers may help them to form such a group. The key to the success and effectiveness of these groups is the sharing of ideas, support and feedback among members.

Task group is a term used by social workers and also by organizational management experts. The term refers to the groups formed to accomplish specific tasks. They may be formed to meet client needs, organizational needs or community needs (Toseland and Rivas, 2001). In India a large number of social workers work with large scale organizations and with a variety of employees. A command group is a term given to a group, which has a formal head or leader and a specific number of persons are placed under her/him to accomplish any given objective.

A *therapy group* is formed for providing support to members to achieve solutions to mental health related issues. Therapy groups help members change their behaviour, cope with personal problems or rehabilitate themselves after a trauma, etc. Therapy groups make a significant use of group experiences of members for changing sensitivity levels and feeling patterns of the individual to enhance the coping mechanisms or reformulate the coping strategies.

Single session group is a term used to refer to groups that serve new members at each meeting. Although one or two persons may attend more than one single session group, the composition of the group is likely to be different from one session to the next (see Kosoff, 2003).

Peer group refers to members in the same age group or occupational category coming together to enjoy each other's company. It may or may not meet very regularly.

Reference group is a term used by sociologists to refer to groups which are valued by individuals for developing their own values, attitudes and behaviour patterns. In forming their attitudes and beliefs and in performing their actions, people will compare or identify themselves with other people or other groups of people whose attitude, beliefs and actions are taken as appropriate.

Other terms associated with group work practice are recreational groups, treatment groups and those referring to specific clients such as children's groups, youth groups, women's groups or groups of elderly persons. Similarly, farmer's groups or workers groups are also terms of common usage.

As Brown (1997) noted, there are many ways leading to the formation of a group. While some form spontaneously, others may be part of an agency programme. Still others may come together on the initiative of a worker. The members may join voluntarily or they may be coerced or persuaded. There may be some planning for the formation. In some cases the formation may be a long drawn process while in others, groups may form more quickly. Brown noted the following points of working with groups:

1. The small group is a reflection of the larger society and may have features of inequality;
2. The use of social interaction among members to achieve group goals is the key;
3. It is an empowering method as all members are helped. At the same time they are helpers as well. Thus groups are powerful instruments of change;

4. The key variables in group are: context, group dynamics, individual members and the worker.

Another aspect that we need to understand about the group is what factors facilitate the integration of group, help in the commencement of common activities and lead to the emergence of a group consciousness. Group integration follows different lines but family, kinship and other primordial ties such as tribal, caste, regional, linguistic and religious affinities are natural sources of integration. Yet the struggle for power and consequently a need to dominate over other members is found even in the most primary groups based on close relationships. In the context of a large group, smaller groups based on these ties are commonly found. However, we are concerned here with groups which are formed for meeting needs of various kinds and which are different from the groups that spontaneously emerge. The major integrating factor in such groups is therefore the need or the purpose for which the group is formed. Other factors that are likely to affect the functioning of the groups are its size, the difference of attitudes, values and general personality traits among individual members, and effective leadership, etc. (see Mills, 1967).

Social Work Group

In social work a group refers to a collection of members varying in number from 8 to 15 generally (please note there is no formula to determine the size), either formed by a social worker or voluntarily through the initiative of one or more members. The purpose in keeping the group small in size is to be able to monitor the progress of each member in the group.

Manheim (1957) looked at the group as a social force trying to integrate individuals. The main characteristics of groups he identified are: a relative organization meaning some kind of division of roles and functions among members; group norms, ideas about existence or purpose of group and its relationship with other groups; collective interest and individual interest; a system of distributing power; and repressions and conflicts and mechanisms to deal with them.

Studies of Groups

The search for laws or a framework to explain the functioning of groups in social work began as early as 1930 when Grace Coyle studied social process in an organized group as her doctoral research project.

Her formulation included the process of group formation, membership selection, goal development, structural arrangement, leadership, creation of bond, group culture, group control and collective thinking. A report based on research with actual groups by Stein and Newcomb in 1938, dealt with concepts such as bond, interaction, status and so on, and suggested that individuals can grow through group associations.

Another study of group by Newcomb (1943) revealed that a group influenced the attitudes of the members and that the degree of influence of the group on the individual depended to a large degree on the relationship of the individual with the group and that groups evaluate, rank and reward members. Sherif's study in 1936 has indicated how the group influenced the member's perception of reality and how individual members influenced the group norms.

Similarly, Bales (1950) contributed significantly in studying the interaction process in the group. He was the first to identify that a group engaged in work or task related activities along with efforts to maintain the emotional responses of the members in the group. Both set of activities were vital for the smooth functioning of a group. He also pointed out that a group goes through different stages or phases in its process of organization or problem solving. The scale he developed to measure whether a group is task-oriented or person-oriented is a very useful tool in understanding a group. The study of group dynamics by Cartwright and Zander (1968), focused on concepts such as composition of membership cohesion, pressure to uniformity, power, influence and motivation, etc. The studies provided a framework for group work practice, to use group as a medium to induce changes in the individuals, groups and communities and to accomplish other objectives.

Group Effect on Participants

Cooley (1909), one of the earliest group theorists, postulated that it was by group experience that the individual becomes socialized. According to him, socialization is "the sequence of social learning experiences that result in the integration of the individual into a society." Social learning implies that the individual takes on values, norms, acceptable behaviour, and life style through interaction with others. This process seems to be most influenced by small groups: family, friendships, peers, school groups, play groups, occupational groups and associational groups. Cooley (1909) said that a group is a medium and the context for producing changes in members that endure beyond the existence of the group. These changes, he said, appear in attitudes, personality traits, interests, or skills, and occur during and after interaction among members of a group.

Cartwright (1961) observed that the "behaviour, attitudes, beliefs and values of the individual are all firmly grounded in groups to which he belongs." "What he believes to be true and good, whom he loves and hates, what beliefs and prejudices he holds, are highly influenced by his group membership." Cartwright concludes that "whether [people] change or resist change will be influenced by their groups."

Helanko (1963) found age nine to be specially significant for joining groups. Around this age he noted, children learn to behave in primary groups in the company of their equals such as neighbourhood boys or school groups, with strong solid in-group feelings and strong, internal pull for the members. The period between nine to twelve years he characterized with intensive interaction in a closed circle, and firm organization repellent to others in groups numbering six or seven.

Identity and Self-Concept

Not only values, beliefs, and behaviour develops from interaction with others, but an individual's impression of self and an assessment of his own worth, also develops from association with others.

Mead (1934) theorized that a person's perception of self came almost totally from the image the person perceived in the responses of others to him or her. He wrote of the "looking-glass self" – the self one sees reflected in the way others respond to him. He also wrote of the "significant others" in one's life – those people who take on meaning for one and influence one's impression of self. Although his sense of adequacy may come from his actual successes and failures in achievement, his standards of expectation for himself are culturally derived from the expectation of those significant others in his life. The responses that he receives from those about him give him some measure of himself. A person is apt to approve those factors in himself that others approve, and disapprove of those features for which he is criticized.

In an effort to test Mead's theory, Manis (1955) studied men in small living groups in residences and discovered that over time a person's conception of himself tended to change in the direction of others' expectations of him. The group did not modify its expectations of the man. Revisions in the person's self-perception tended to be an improvement in evaluation of self, and the change was more greatly influenced by opinions of friends or people who had significant meaning to him, than by people who knew him but were not close personal friends.

Sears and Sherman (1964) also conducted studies on the origins of self-approval and found evidence that self-evaluation stemmed from responses of others and standards set by significant others. They found that over a period of time "changes in children's physical development, scholastic achievement and socially desirable behaviour were closely related to differential treatment by teachers, peers, and families, and this in turn resulted in considerable change in self-esteem."

Golembiewski (1962) theorized similarly that "friendships and affections are available often only in group interaction. A person's conception of self and the preservation of that self-conception are very often group products. These gratifications attract people to groups." He suggested further that groups provide a frame of reference or an anchor for the individual and his behaviour. If one's sense of self derives from one's contacts in various associations and groups, movement into and among various social groups in which there are different expectations of a person, might result in role conflicts and confusions. McDavid and Harrari (1968) suggest that "to the extent that participation in groups introduces varied new elements into the self-concept, internal conflicts within ..... the self-concept are likely to increase as the number of group identifications in which the person engages increase." On the other hand, if a person with many associations synthesizes the many expectations of himself in his various associations, he broadens and strengthens his self-image.

The formation of self-image and social behaviour not only derives from group experiences throughout life, but also can be modified and made more socially effective through guided group experience (Lewin, 1951). Changes in the person from this experience are thought to be cognitive and to include increased self-awareness, emotionally changed attitudes, and behaviourally changed interpersonal competence, according to Schein and Bennis (1965).

Values and Attitudinal Change

As suggested in the socializing process, a person's sense of right and wrong, good and bad, true and false, develops from those around him/her. Initially, these cultural attributes come from the family but they are later shaped by other sources such as playgroups, peer groups, and throughout life from significant others in the reference groups.

"When an individual is in a social situation he tends to react toward others in the same way that he thinks others would react to him," according to Mead. This behavioural effect of the social situation gives indication of considerable group influence on an individual's functioning. One may observe in family discussion, committee deliberations, and conversations among friends where people are merely expressing themselves, that people tend to move toward the collective group opinion. Some of the factors that will affect group influence upon the member and vice versa are: the significance of a particular group in relation to other groups of which the individual is a member; the amount of attachment a person has to other people in the group; the type of group culture, that is, group values and norms; the status of the person in the particular group; and the rewards for conformity or the sanctions for nonconformity in the particular group.

The individual not only acquires his values and beliefs in his associations, but Cartwright and Lippitt (1961) found that "the individual needs social support for his values and social beliefs." They felt that he needs to be accepted as a valid person, as a member of the group he values. Failure to maintain such a group membership produces anxiety and personal disorganization. On the other hand, group membership and participation cost the person his individuality – if he is going to receive support he must give support and hold some common values and beliefs. Lewin (1951) makes a similar observation when he says "when an individual tries to diverge too much from group standards he will be ridiculed, treated severely, and finally ousted from the group."

Changes in Groups

We have thus far focused on the influence of group experience upon members and the possibility of groups created for purposes of development and change of person or persons. What are the possibilities of intervening in groups that already exist? Lewin (1943) considered the effects of attempting change in autonomous groups, or groups already existing within society. Gangs, friendship groups, autonomous cliques or subgroups within institutions or other wider associations often appear. When the members have formed the group autonomously, what are the possibilities for inducing changes in the group?

Lewin suggests that as attempts to change an individual outside of his group may make him a deviant, it would be more advisable to change the group level of values, behaviours, or beliefs. This process can take place through discussion and decision-making in the group. A clear idea of a new kind of behaviour or activity may help in the task. The group as a whole, therefore, must change, and in that process the individual members will not only change, but reinforce each other in the change.

Lewin postulates that where there is an enduring group with relatively high interaction, the individual would have higher commitment to the group than to others outside; therefore, it would be easier to change the behaviour of the individuals as a group than to change them one by one. He suggests further that when it seems impossible to change the standards of an entire group, a small segment may be formed or worked with. Lewin found it was necessary to insulate them from the larger group, the neighbourhood of delinquents or the social circles of alcoholics, in order to reduce the forces that supported the individual's behaviour at the old level.

The concept of 'cultural island' emerged from this research. Specifically, some of the people were removed from their surroundings to a camp, workshop, or other group, where their changes were reinforced over a period of time in the new group setting in a special therapeutic or change-related subculture so that the modified standards or behaviours could be reinforced long enough to become incorporated in the habits of the individual member. The pressure of some of his other reference group members helped a subgroup to build in supports for the individual's return to the original, now alien, culture. This process has been attempted with youth leaders from colleges, schools, and isolated segregated communities to give an experience in intercultural and international living and modify biases and prejudices.

Lippitt et al. (1958) added to Lewin's theory of group training and retraining, the suggestion that when two or more people are retrained together they constitute a subgroup in which the newly learned attitudes and activities constitute a group standard and they reinforce each other in retaining the change. Berelson and Steiner (1964) also support the idea of group change through an interaction process as opposed to individual change. They said that active discussion by a small group to determine goals, to choose methods of work, to reshape operations, or to solve problems, is more effective in changing group practice than separate instruction to individual members. Group activity, they think, brings about better motivation and support for change and better implementation and productivity of new practice.

Coach and French (1948) found in their research in industry, that where workers were encouraged to participate in group deliberation and decision-making around change in procedures, there was less expression of aggression to supervisors, less drop in production, and quicker recovery from any production drop, less quitting, and a higher final rate of production. When orders were handed down from above with no group participation, and no suggestions or feedback, there was considerable grumbling, some work stoppages, absenteeism, and slowdown in production. Bavelas (1942) similarly found that while encouragement and incentives from management did not improve individual piecework production rate, a group decision by workers after discussion did result in improvement. Such findings offer strong support for engaging people in group deliberation and for the effect of group contagion on individual and group performances.

Task Groups for Problem-Solving

The use of groups for problem solving is another area in which there has been theoretical formulation and research. The question frequently arises as to whether individuals working alone or in groups are more effective in finding solutions to problems. There is no theory which can satisfactorily answer the question. Group problem solving is a process whereby people work together to contribute individually and collectively to a common solution for some problem. Some differences are apparent between the problems which lend themselves to group solutions and those which do not. For instance, Hare (1962) concluded in a survey of considerable research on problem solving, that "the superiority of the group over the individual with respect to productivity is usually greater on manual problems than on intellectual tasks." He found that the group lost its superiority in accuracy and efficiency if no division of labour was required, if the group had to spend too much time and energy on its own development and control, or if the group level of productivity was lower than that of the separate individuals. Furthermore, group problem solving generally took more time for the same amount of return as individual activity. Groups tended to be more accurate because of the greater number of checks and balances. After group deliberation over a problem, the individual member tended to be more accurate in his own judgment. Recall is greater for groups than individuals, because there seem to be more resources for memory in the group.

In groups it is important to remember that all members do not carry equal power or prestige. There is a general tendency among people to side with people in power or remain silent even if they do not agree with the decision. When a group is in deliberation and attempting to arrive at a group solution to a problem, alternatives are presented and there emerges a process of decision-making in which various alternatives are rejected until one alternative is finally selected. Unless there is some provision for minority expression, opinions that differ from the final alternative selected may get lost in the final group decision.

Group problem-solving, therefore, has its benefits and its disadvantages. Whether the group process is superior to individual problem solving depends to some degree on the nature of the problem and the desired outcome. Another factor of the decision regarding group or individual is, who will be responsible for implementing the outcomes or putting the suggested solution into effect. If the solution is going to affect the group and implies changes in procedures, the engagement of those who will be affected by the solution may ensure greater acceptance if the members determine the solution. Lessons may be drawn for the uses of groups in administration, community organization and planning, coordination of services, and other task-focused groups in social work practice.

Change in System

The group can be used as a means for changing social structures and institutions in which it exists. The organization of groups or the use of groups in this way suggests social or political action. The theory suggests that strength from number of people in collective action has an effect on a target institution or organization. That is, in the political processes, many people speaking and acting collectively, or in an organized fashion, may have greater influence than individuals speaking separately. The group attempting external change, or affecting changes in a system of which it is a part, will have to give some attention to its own development. In order for the group to take up the task, members will need to work together and be able to engage in deliberations as a group. Furthermore, the group must have enough clarity and cohesion of opinion on how to modify the external system.

While considerable research has been done on the internal workings of groups and the group as an instrument for growth and change in individuals, and while social scientists have stated that the group is the link between the individual and the wider society, there seems to have been very little theory building or research on the group as an instrument for modification of the wider society.

Some of the principles to be considered in the use of the group for change of a wider social system as indicated by Bennis, Benne, and Chin (1961) are as follows:

1. The members must be able to function well enough as individuals and collectively to constitute a group that provides a unified force for action.
2. The group must be synthesized enough to support its members against the external resistance to change that generally appears as a reaction.
3. The group must provide rewards for the members from within the group if their proposed change means deviance from the wider social system and the possibility of negative social sanctions in the wider society or external system.
4. In order to change a system the group must have access to strategic people or subgroups in it.
5. Resources (both financial and informational) must be available for the group to take the necessary action to be forceful and effective in moving toward its target for action.
6. Generally, it is thought to be essential for exerting influence to change a system, to have access to the news media and other channels of communication and information, in order to gain recognition and support.

It is recognized in the political arena that well-organized numbers of people with a unified outlook do carry political influence especially if they give evidence of being representative of others (Truman, 1951).

In other words, the power of organization and representation is well accepted. The inclusion of people who have prestige as group members whose eminence derives from sources outside the group, use of bloc voting, the organization of minority groups, and the use of mechanisms, such as demonstrations, work stoppages, engaging the public media to gain public recognition or make an administration's position uncomfortable, are measures to gain or exercise influence that may be used by an organized group. The target for change may be formal organizations or institutions, such as schools, police, agencies, or governmental structures, or, in contrast, less-organized structures, such as neighbourhoods, apartment houses, or communities.

Just as task-centred groups may evolve into personally satisfying social groups, social organizations formed for purposes of action outside the group may tend to lose sight of their original goals. People may gain more satisfaction from belonging to the group than in getting the job done. Thus one might say, the structure of the organization may come to outweigh the goals for which it was created.

When a group is sufficiently organized to take action and has achieved its goals, it is likely not to want to dissolve but rather to go on to new goals. The effectiveness of the organization and the morale achieved by group accomplishment gives momentum to further activity. Furthermore, in working together on their problems, the members may form strong attachments to each other and to the group. The small group organized for purposes of external action may become formally organized in order to achieve the action. The result is the creation of an organization within an organization, system, or institution.

It has been suggested, however, that, "the efficiency of a large formal organization is sizably enhanced when ... [its operations] are tied into the informal network of groups within [it] so that this network can be used to support the organization goals" (Berelson and Steiner, 1964). In other words, the small group can be the bridge from the person to the larger organization, as well as the means by which the larger organization operates or is changed.

The operation of informal groups in a large system works two ways. While on the one hand the groups may come into being to bring about change in their surroundings, to affect the system and the wider organization, they may in turn be used by the system to modify the participants and to acculturate them to the pressures and goals of the wider system. The informal group can be effectively used in translating, interpreting, and supporting the organization's norms and practices. Leighton (1945) noted that, "communication from a central authority to a community works much better if conducted through the informally selected leaders of the basic social units set up by the residents."

Most of the research and line of reasoning about small groups for purposes of social action and social change, seems to focus on the internal workings of the group and the effect of the system on modifying the group, rather than on the processes by which the small group, when organized, may change society or the wider social system. Any group taking action formulates its action on the basis of an interpretation and assessment of the situation. People perceive a current situation in light of their previous life experiences. Members of a group composed of people of diverse backgrounds will be inclined to define the situation differently according to their various frames of reference resulting in considerable strain. Although there are theoretical differences between the social science theorists on whether the social situation is the cause, the effect, or the setting of social change, they agree that the people in the small group who wish to effect change in their social conditions must be closely related to their target for change, that is, they must have positions in the system they wish to change.

If the group is to be effective in bringing about some change in the system or organization in which it exists, or if it is to have any effect on some other institutions, the group members themselves must be engaged in the process and committed to the purposes for which the group exists. Sometimes leadership, either staff or organizational, recognizes the existence of a problem or a situation which needs to be remedied. They then organize committees or task forces to work on a solution. However, the leadership may have already decided on procedures and solutions or expected outcomes. The expectations from the newly organized group is that it will give total support to the plans, procedures, and goals set by the organizer. This procedure is a dubious use of the group. In fact, it is of no use to the group itself. If people are to be involved on their own behalf or in an activity to achieve some specific end, then they need to be fully engaged in deliberation and decisions about the direction of the activity, and their decisions and recommended outcomes must be respected. For example, Thelen (1954) working with depressed neighbourhoods, organized block clubs to train their own leadership. People in interaction with each other developed mutuality of feeling where there had been alienation and anomie. They also reduced the differences in the ways people looked at some problems and came to some agreements on solution, and engaged more people in working on the solution, thus removing some of the external depression.

Personality Variables

Various kinds of personality variables have been examined with regard to group composition and group functioning. Based on an assessment of individual characteristics such as intellectual capacity, adjustment, extroversion and introversion, masculinity and feminity, and like factors, attempts have been made to predict how a person will behave in a group. The behaviour tendencies which a person may show on an individual basis when tested alone may be different from his/ her actual behaviour when s/he is in the presence of others or is interacting with them. A person who tends to be aggressive and has leadership qualities which enables her/ him to assume responsibility for any group may restrain himself in a situation where s/he is in the presence of high status people whom s/he wishes to impress with her/his affability, or who may be more competitive than her/himself.

Schutz (1958), in an effort to predict compatibility of people in group functioning, developed some measures of personality on predictable interactional qualities. His test, called FIRO (Fundamental Interpersonal Relations Orientation), measured three dimensions of an individual's potential behaviour with others: personalness, power, and assertiveness. Personalness or counter-personalness refers to the individual's capacity to move into close personal relationships, getting people to like her/ him, being a "good guy" and treating people differentially, as opposed to keeping people removed and at a distance, remaining aloof or appearing indifferent. The power orientation refers to ways of relating to authority, taking on authority, following rules, following the leader, conforming to manipulation or controlling the power structure. The assertiveness orientation refers to the predisposition to express one self openly in interpersonal relations or to withhold expression. On the basis of a test of these qualities, profiles are constructed for each individual, and people are grouped with similar profiles. These groupings are referred to as compatible. People grouped on the basis of mixed profiles were referred to as incompatible. It was found that people with similar profiles were more compatible than people with widely diverse profiles. For instance, people who were considered personable and were grouped together created a more compatible group, and people who were considered counter-personable, were more compatible and operated better together than the mixture of both personable/counter-personable.

Groups composed of people with similar interpersonal qualities attained higher cohesion, maintained a more permissive and supportive group atmosphere, and their members were more strongly attracted to the group and to each other. Incompatible groups, composed of people with dissimilar traits, lacked focus, shifted leadership and frequently gave up.

Cattell (1948) developed a sixteen-factor personality test to show the presence of such characteristics as vigour, dominance, adventure-someness, suspiciousness, nervous tension, emotional immaturity, and many others. Experiments were performed composing groups of persons with various ratings on Cattell's tests, in order to determine whether the combination of people with similarity or variance of ratings on these tests might predict to group performance. Cattell and associates introduced the concept of group syntality, meaning the internal synthesis of a group or the group's functioning as an entity, which produced the capacity of the group members to perform together. Since no two persons would probably have identical personality profiles, they used group means on each personality variable rather than a combined rating. They also made combinations of variables related to certain group synergy states. They found, for instance, that groups that showed task performance at a high level of coordination, such as doing things together, which was preferred over discussion, resulted from a group in which there were high group means on vigour, dominance, adventure-someness, purposefulness, orderliness, self-determination and freedom from anxiety. Groups where there were high group means on suspiciousness, tension, immaturity, anxiety, and lack of self-sufficiency showed high frustration, lack of leadership, lack of order and *"we feeling,"* low motivation, and little organization and inter-dependence.

When members showed high group means on friendliness, intelligence, level of radicalism, along with variances on such factors as talkativeness, enjoying carefree excitement, and fast repartee and variance on social norms, their groups showed a high level of accuracy on tasks requiring a judgment of fact from inferences. They also showed a controlled group atmosphere. Groups where there was considerable uniformity in emotional maturity were characterized as being optimistic and having confidence in their achievement aspirations.

Implications of Social Science Research for Group Work

Social group work practice based on the above findings relating to small groups has developed the following assumptions:

- Group is a powerful source for influencing the behaviour of its members;
- Group is a potential source for meeting individual needs;
- Group dynamics can be planned and structured to achieve desirable results; and
- The group can be used for meeting community needs or achieving changes in the community.

Within social work practice, groups are effectively used to support individuals in growth, rehabilitation, personal change, and for prevention of social and personal breakdown. A group can also be used for the development and change of the group's own environment, for modifying systems, and for changing some of the institutions of society. While experience in social work practice has produced evidence that certain ends can be achieved through practice with groups, there has been relatively little research to establish empirically that group methods produce expected results. In India particularly, such efforts have been missing. Social work literature, especially descriptions of practice, conclude that some problems are amenable to treatment or change through group activity, without providing adequate data. Groups have been largely used as means of service delivery for social development, such as preparation for new experiences, teaching or changing values, modification of life style, problem solving, community and social planning, and many other purposes.

Research on groups has produced evidence of the effects of groups in influencing certain results. Individuals undergo change in a group, and changes can be induced in a system, community or society. While for any member a group may have a primary or stated purpose or use, there usually may be other purposes which are hidden or unstated. Groups usually have similar purposes as a whole. The group goals and purposes and individual goals and purposes may undergo change. A group may have different meanings for members through time; the purpose or goals and their usefulness may increase or decrease. Motivation of members affects goal orientation and has a vital impact on psychological and behavioural process. Emotional state, learning and problem solving strategies, including the process of perception of facts and situation analysis are directly affected by motivation and goal orientation. Yet, so far it remains a complex and undefined area. The interaction in a group and group dynamics is still being researched, as a group has to invest a lot of energy in managing some members, while other members contribute a great deal in keeping the group together. The group has power over members and is in a position to resolve many issues. Yet, not all groups are successful in dealing with deviance. Napier and Gershenfeld (2004) described power of the group in terms of conformity, compliance, and obedience on the part of members. They noted that group members accept group norms since:

- They value membership of the group;
- The members feel that their status is enhanced as a result of group membership;
- The cohesiveness of the group is a valuable experience for members; and
- The group has the power to sanction members and their behaviour.

Social science theoretical formulations and studies therefore permit us to propose the following categories of group use:

Where the focus is on members: socialization-re-socialization, acquiring or changing concept of self, identity, motivation; attitude formation and change, formation and modification of values and beliefs; behavioural change; achieving a sense of belonging and support; education;

Where the focus is task orientation: economic activities, social tasks or awareness generation particularly about group, community or social situation;

For change in social situation or conditions outside the group: (a) modification of the institution or social system within which the group exists; or (b) of the social situation – including the community or society – through pressure, dissemination of information, or organization; modification of attitudes of outsiders (Hartford, 1972).

These have implications for group uses toward the specific ends of socialization and teaching of values and norms at specific ages. For instance, an effort to organize groups of nursery-age children may be futile, while small groups of children from ages seven on may be useful if the purpose of the group is socialization and the development of self-control and self-managed groups. They also suggest guidelines for working with people who have suffered social deprivations or interruptions of normal social development due to physical or emotional handicaps or illnesses. There are possibilities for re-socialization or modification of internalized roles from a subsystem of society, such as use of groups for the modification of racist attitudes, delinquent behaviour, or other antisocial lifestyles.

3

Assumptions and Theories Helpful in Working with Groups

Life Skills

One of the frameworks used in working with group is the assumption that many persons lack the requisite skills and experiences to cope with stresses in their social relationships. These stresses usually occur in their childhood when children and adolescents move from one status and role position to the other or from one interaction milieu to the other. For example, when a child moves out from a relatively contained, secure and static home environment to a school which is a more open and dynamic environment, from a primary school to middle or higher secondary school, from school to college, etc. These changes create stress as a child or an adolescent is expected to adopt to a new set of norms and also rules, meant for regulating behaviour. Adolescents in general experience stress associated with physical development, social acceptance and academic performance. The degree of stress is directly related to the degree of change they experience in the new setting, and the life skills they possess in coping with the change. For example, for a young boy to move from a rural school to an urban higher education institution will cause more stress than for a young person moving from an urban school to a higher education institution in an urban area. Similarly, a child from a family of uneducated parents will face more stress at school and other educational institutions. The inadequacy of life skills such as verbal and non verbal communication, asserting, handling feelings and conflicts, coupled with experience of functioning in a group consisting of members from a multicultural background, increases the stress leading to maladjustment problems. This framework helps a group worker to understand the children and adolescents exhibiting stress symptoms and their inability to adjust in the group. The worker can provide these children a support group to discuss their problems and learn from each other and to understand the coping strategies that they are using to deal with the situation. The group worker can also help them to learn new life skills to update their competence to cope with stresses and sources of stresses.

Sharing Feedback

Peer relations greatly influence children and adolescents. Hence, it is important for them to understand how others rate them. The process of nicknaming persons is a common occurrence in all societies and at all stages. Generally, the labels aptly describe how others view the behaviour of a person. The group can provide an opportunity to children and adolescents to discover how others view them. It can also help them to analyze it objectively and learn to take corrective action if needed. For example, if a person is identified as a 'bully', what are its implications, and how can one change the label. A discussion of stereotypes can also be helpful in understanding labels and how to deal with them. There are also instances of giving labels to members of a particular religious, linguistic or caste group, which are negative. The children and adolescents of these groups experience a high degree of stress leading to academic and mental health problems. The group worker can use the knowledge to design a number of programmes for children and adolescents indulging in labeling and for those who are at the receiving end.

Emotional Support

Many persons experience trauma due to a variety of reasons. Some examples are loss of significant persons, family violence, long-term unemployment, retirement trauma, and loss of shelter or other valuables, etc. These conditions produce stress and could become traumatic. Individual counselling is helpful but emotional trauma shared with fellow sufferers has been found to be of help. The studies of children and adolescents affected by disasters indicate that the trauma produces a great deal of anxiety, resulting in loss of concentration and producing incoherent behaviour. The adolescent's reaction to stress may vary such as withdrawal or opting out, depression, loss of control, inability to concentrate, irritability, disturbed sleep or eating patterns, flashbacks and emotional numbing (Carll, 1994). Loss of significant members such as parents or siblings and material resources such as housing will require a different set of life skills and coping strategies to survive. The studies indicate that emotional support from others who have undergone a similar trauma is helpful (Shelby, 1994). The finding is used to form groups of persons having suffered a trauma to provide emotional support to each other.

By now it is clear that in order to understand the events taking place within a group, one needs to understand the individuals within the group on the one hand and their interaction in the group on the other. There are now a number of psychological theories providing an explanation of individual behaviour and how it can help in understanding the group functioning. A number of studies on group psychology and group dynamics are now available to provide important insights about groups.

Psychoanalytic Theory

Freud (1922/66) is perhaps one of the earliest theorists to provide an explanation of human personality. Freud conceptualized that the human mind has two broad systems. One he described as conscious, pre-conscious and unconscious and the other as Id, Ego and Super Ego. Freud suggested that mind was composed of thoughts (ideas), feelings, instincts, drives, conflicts and motives. Most of these elements were located in the unconscious or preconscious. There is a repressed area which serves as a barrier where a lot of disturbing material (thoughts and feelings), as unresolved conflicts, are placed through the process of defense mechanism. Defence mechanism or repression is a process in which unacceptable desires, memories and thoughts are excluded from consciousness by sending the material into the unconscious under the repressed barrier. Freud suggests that this results in producing irritants such as unwanted emotions and behaviour such as anger, hallucinations, etc. Describing the second system Freud explains that Id is the primitive psychic force hidden in the unconscious. It represents the basic needs and drives such as hunger, thirst, sex and self preservation, which support other personality factors. Id governed by the pleasure principle primarily seeks to express itself irrespective of the consequences, while Ego acts as the rational component of the mind which controls the thinking of the mind. Super ego serves as the conscience by indicating what is right and wrong socially and morally. Freud conceptualized that people pass through six psychosocial development stages. During any one of the stages conflicts may arise and if it remains unresolved the person's personality development will be affected. He thought that disturbances can arise from several sources. Traumatic experiences which a person's ego is not able to cope with directly are repressed. Similarly internal unconscious processes could also cause disturbances (see Zastrow and Ashman, 1990). Freud, in elaborating the group's influence on human behaviour, specifically mentions about the importance of group leader, and the early life experiences of the members. The members use transference in their interactions that occur within the group and try to recreate their conflicts and defense mechanisms.

More recent psychoanalytic group treatment have adapted and modified classical psychoanalytic theory to emphasize the current experiences of group interaction. Through direct, mutual interpersonal communications members build interpersonal skills, adaptive capacities and ego strength, and develop self awareness of their behaviour and its implications in a group situation. The cohesiveness of the group helps members to feel secure and able to share the intimate personal details of their life and to act out their conflicts in the safe and supportive environment of the group. For details see the text on Psychoanalytic theory.

A number of psychologists have contributed in developing learning theory as an explanation of human behaviour.

Learning Theory

Learning Theory has created a lot of controversy in group work (Toseland and Rivas, 2001) as it focuses more on individual than on group dynamics with reference to influencing individual behaviour. Learning theory also provides a framework for understanding human behaviour. It provides an understanding of the social functioning of persons within their environments. The person in dynamic interaction with all aspects of the environment is the focus of attention. Further, it emphasizes the importance of assessment of observable behaviour, and advocates the use of specific terms in defining behaviour. And finally it takes a positive approach that if a behaviour is learned then it can also be unlearned.

Respondent conditioning refers to the emission of behaviour in response to a specific stimulus. The stimulus could be a word, sight or a sound. The second type of learning is called modeling, which simply refers to learning by observation. The children of parents who smoke are likely to be smokers. Children of parents with ability to control their feelings under stress are likely to learn self-control. However, a number of factors or conditions can affect the effectiveness of modeling. Some of them are similarity of the model to the observer, the prestige, status and expertise of the model, and the diversity of models around the observer. Operant conditioning is a type of learning in which behaviours are altered primarily by regulating the subsequences which follow them. New behaviours could be learned and undesirable behaviours could be weakened and eliminated by regulating the consequences. By using the learning theory framework, the group can provide reinforcements to strengthen a behaviour. There are both positive and negative reinforcements. A good example of negative reinforcement in a group situation is to discourage a behaviour by booing, if the proper dress code or language or behaviour code is violated. The person will then behave in a particular manner to avoid the booing. However, a more severe response like terminating the membership to weaken a behaviour is called punishment. Similarly extinction or withdrawal of reinforcements result in weakening of particular behaviour. The learning theory thus provides a framework for group workers to modify behaviour. The context could be achievement of group tasks and development, or helping the members to unlearn behaviours that create problems in their social functioning.

Sociologists have also studied groups and their functioning. They have come up with a number of interesting findings that are helpful in highlighting the functioning of groups.

Field Theory

Kurt Lewin (1946) was one of the pioneers to scientifically study group functioning. He focused on the forces that influenced the working of groups. He and his colleagues tried to study leadership styles by creating groups with different styles of leaderships in order to see their impact on the functioning of the group. It is commonly observed that a leader becomes authoritarian when the members are seeking favours, rather than questioning the decisions or even discussing the issues objectively. Lewin (1946) argued that the leadership style is a product of leader member interaction rather than a personality trait of the leader. Further, Lewin, while developing his Field Theory, argued that a group has a life space and it has movement. It tries to accomplish goals or group tasks and faces hurdles in its movement (locomotion). Lewin believed that group was an entity of opposing forces which keep the group members in the group and move them along in achieving group goals. However, the behaviour of individual members and the group itself should be seen as a product of the totality of the group situation (Lewin, 1946).

Lewin (1946) introduced several concepts to help in the understanding of forces at work in the group. Some of them are: (a) *Roles* – status rights and duties of group members; (b) *Norms* – rules governing the behaviour of group members; (c) *Power* – the ability of members to influence one another; (d) *Cohesion* – the attraction the group members feel towards one another and towards the group; (e) *Consensus* – the degree of agreement regarding goals and other group phenomena; and (f) *Valence* – the potency of goals and objects in the life space of the group. Other field theorists have continued to work on the characteristics of group that influence the individual behaviour. Cohesion has been identified as an important factor, defined as, *"the totality of forces acting on individual members to keep them in the group"*. Cohesion reflects the agreement on goals and norms, shared understanding and a greater homogeneity in demographic background, as also the productivity, satisfaction and cooperative interaction patterns (Cartwright and Zander, 1968).

Lewin developed t-group as a means to observe the effects of group processes on group members and as a means to induce changes in behaviour. Lewin thus helped in developing a theory that people change when they see their behaviour as others see it, thus leading to development of the feedback method whereby the group members and the group leader provide feedback to the individual as to how his/her behaviour was affecting them. Role plays and simulations are also used to highlight the group process. The group workers using the field theory framework can design their own interventions in working with the group for achieving the group goals along with individual development.

Systems Theory

Systems Theory is also helpful to explain the functioning of a group. Talcott Parsons (1951) defined social system as a set of interdependent elements trying to function as a unified whole to maintain order and a stable equilibrium. The social systems are constantly facing new challenges as the environment around them and within, is constantly changing. Therefore, they must act to maintain the equilibrium if they have to survive. This act of survival depends upon four basic functions: (a) integration; (b) adaptation; (c) pattern maintenance; and (d) goal attainment. The group viewed as a system would therefore be able to achieve its objectives if it is able to carry out these four functions effectively. It is able to integrate members by achieving individual and group goal matching. It also has the capacity to make changes to adapt itself to outside demands like that of the community and the sponsoring organization and with the internal dynamics as it changes with time. The pattern maintenance would require development of norms and guidelines to regulate its activities and develop well defined objectives, identity and procedures, that are able to sustain these over time. The functioning of a system depends to a great extent on the clarity about these functions and the members get into a set pattern of carrying out the role assigned to them. The goal attainment is the final task to ensure the smooth functioning of the system. The members will lose interest and the functioning of the group will be affected if the goals are not being achieved. The faith of the members that the group goals are attainable is an important attribute of group stability and functioning. Parsons pointed out that problems will arise during the functioning of the group; the group, including its leadership must make use of its resources effectively to tackle the problems to maintain the equilibrium of the group.

Robert Bales (1950), however, believed that the survival of the group depends on two central tasks. The first he termed the instrumental problems related to tasks or goal related functions and the second, socio-emotional tasks related to the interpersonal relationships between members, and between members and leader, for coordinating and maintaining the emotional unity and morale of the group. While the instrumental problems generally arise on account of the external pressures, the socio emotional problems are rooted in the internal dynamics of the group. The insights are helpful for workers to deal with both kinds of challenges in their working with groups. It is often seen that exclusive focus on one results in ignoring the other, making the group dysfunctional in the process. However, Bales sees this as natural, as the group struggles to maintain a dynamic equilibrium between the two sets of functions. Bales prefers a certain amount of tension and antagonism to Parsons' emphasis on harmony. The worker can keep in mind that the emphasis on tasks will vary in different groups, depending upon the central purpose of the group. It will be different in a self-help group formed to achieve a specific task, than in a group of children. It is also possible to analyze the interaction between members in a group by using a tool developed by Bales called Interaction Process Analysis.

Conflict Theory

Although sociologists differ in their understanding of conflict as a social phenomenon in society, yet some of the explanations of conflicts are helpful in understanding the conflicts in groups and in dealing with them.

Sociologists have identified two broad categories of conflict:

1. *Endogenous conflict:* this refers to sources of changes from within a society
2. *Exogenous conflict:* this refers to changes from without or between systems

Endogenous conflict highlights the following sources of conflict:

1. Inherent predilection to change
2. Conflict over the differential distribution of resources such as wealth, power, and prestige
3. Conflict of values.
4. Conflict of authority
5. Conflict between individual and collectivity

The exogenous conflict identifies three sources:

1. Wars
2. Cultural invasion
3. Conflict of ideology

Lewis Coser (1973) distinguishes between realistic and non-realistic conflicts. Realistic conflicts are conflicts arising on account of non-fulfilment of specific demands, whereas non-realistic conflicts are rooted in the need for release of tension and are not oriented towards achievement of any specific demand.

Function of Social Conflict

In every group there are occasions for conflict, since individuals and sub-groups are likely to make rival claims to scarce resources, prestige or power positions. But social structures differ in the way the group allows expression to these claims. Some are more tolerant, others are not. Closely built groups are likely to suppress conflict. The feeling of hostility tends to accumulate and intensify and when it breaks out it will be intense. This is because of two factors. Firstly, it will not aim at resolving the immediate issue as all accumulated grievances will come to fore. Secondly, it is because of total personality involvement of the group members. It is important for a group worker to remember that the hostility should not be permitted to accumulate and conflict should be allowed to occur wherever a resolution of tension seems to be indicated. In such cases the conflict is likely to remain focused primarily on the condition leading to its outbreak. Conflicts within a group can also help to revitalize existing norms and help to develop new norms as well.

Exchange Theory

The central concern of the exchange theory is to find an explanation for the human transactions of giving and receiving. James Frazer suggests that men enter into institutionalized patterns of exchange to satisfy their economic needs. Malinowski (1944), however, pointed out the difference between economic exchange and social exchange. He further argued that social exchange processes yield for the larger society a moral code of behaviour, which acquires an independent existence outside the social exchange situation and which informs all social, economic, and political interpersonal relationships in society. The triple obligations of social exchange – to give, to receive, and to repay – are to be understood not as self-interest but in terms of interpersonal, hence inter-group, relations. Social exchange transaction creates social bonds creating ties between individuals and the collectivity. Levi-Strauss (1958) argued that it is the exchange which is important not the things which are exchanged and that primary function of the exchange is structural integration of the collectivity (see Ekeh, 1974).

Homans (1961) and Blau (1964) among others have developed the exchange theory to explain members' behaviour within a group.

They argued that all members in a group will try to maximize individual rewards and minimize punishments. All human interaction according to them are seeking something in return from the other. The behaviour is conditioned to maximize rewards and minimize punishment in all interactions. However, the process requires taking decisions and carrying out tasks assigned. Deviations occur as members do not attempt to maximize rewards, which create difficulties in accepting the exchange theory. The cognitive process and the members capacities are not fully explained by the exchange theory. Yet it can serve as a reference point to analyse the behaviour of members in the group. Some of the points of exchange theory can be summarized as follows: Social behaviour is an exchange of goods, material and non-material, such as approval or prestige. Persons that give to others try to get something in return, and persons who receive from others are under pressure to give in return. This process of exchange tends to create an equilibrium to balance the exchanges.

Power Dependence Relations

Emerson (1964) sought to advance exchange theory by developing a theory of power dependence. Emerson attempts to provide a link among the concepts of *'Power'*, *'Authority'*, *'Legitimacy'* and *'Structure'* by giving a definition of power that emphasizes its relational character. He sees power as bound with ties of mutual dependence. This means that 'B's power is proportionally related to 'A's dependence on 'B' for particular rewards or resources. Power is a phenomenon that is realized through social exchange. The explanation can help the group workers to understand the relationship among members in a group. It can also explain the emergence of leadership in a group, and the processes of dominance and obedience. One of the ways of coping with the power of a person is the emotional withdrawal by the other. The other strategy is to extend your networking, by enlisting the support of other persons having a dependence on the same person. For example if 'A' is the dominating person in the group who makes demands on others, 'B' and 'C' join together to balance the power dependence relations. Such networking or coalition formation go on changing as the power dependence relation between members continue to change. The stabilization of this can result in development of group norms and role prescriptions. Both are collective efforts at giving some kind of legitimacy to power dependence relations as also balancing them for the survival of the collective goals. Status ordering also is a balancing act of power dependence relations within group. Some of the salient features of the theory are:

1. Conformity varies directly with motivational investment in the group.
2. Conformity varies inversely with acceptance in alternative groups.
3. Conformity is high at both ends, i.e. the highly valued and the lowly valued members.
4. Coalition of weak members is inevitably formed to control the strong within a coalition.
5. Greatest rewards within a coalition are given to the least dependent member of the coalition. (Emerson, 1964)

Human Capital and Social Capital

James Coleman (1988) is one of the advocates of rational choice theory. Coleman believes in a concept known as 'methodological individualism'. The two concepts in Coleman's theory are actors and resources and the two key resources are: human capital and social capital. Similar to the creation of physical capital by shaping the material into tools and machines to facilitate production, human capital is created by shaping the individuals by giving them skills and capabilities that gives them power to act in innovative ways to produce. Social capital is created by shaping relations between individuals to facilitate action. For example, a group where members trust each other will act better than the one where there is no trust. The importance of social capital has been exhibited by the acceptance of team development efforts by the corporations.

Human capital and social capital can complement each other or they can destroy each other. Social capital as a concept can help the actors to realize the importance and usefulness of those aspects of social structure which will help them to achieve their interests. In a cohesive group where members are willing to help each other and abide by the group norms, the level of trustworthiness of the group environment is a crucial factor in the success of the group. It means that the obligations will be repaid. A simple example is the rotating credit groups. In such groups, each member contributes an amount to a central fund, which is given to a member. Each member gets his/her amount back and in addition gets a loan without interest. However, if obligations and expectations are not balanced the social capital gets diluted. Norms and effective sanction can help in balancing obligations and expectations. The stability of marriage and family in India is an example of effective sanctions, as deviations bring about spontaneous and complete rejection from the entire group, forcing compliance from members.

Social group work practice based on the above findings relating to small groups has developed the following assumptions:

- Group is a powerful source for influencing the behaviour of its members.
- The nature of influence depends on a number of factors such as the size of the group, bond among members, and the capacity of the group to reward members.
- Members carry their social status in the group.
- The internal and external environment of the group is dynamic in nature.
- There are groups within a group.
- Generally members are under pressure to conform to group norms.
- Smaller the group the greater is the intensity of bond between members.
- Group influence on members can be both positive and negative.
- Group is a potential source for meeting individual needs.
- Group dynamics can be planned and structured to achieve desirable results.

4

Group Processes

There are different versions of what the term 'group processes' refers to. Psychologists and group workers of all kinds have tended to talk about 'group processes' – that is a chain of events with a beginning, middle and end sequentially linked, yet it is difficult to identify these (Douglas, 1983). Different authors have identified a number of processes. Douglas further adds that whatever the nature of group processes, any analysis of these should be able to help a worker to use them to exercise some degree of control. We should remember though that the description of what lead a certain process to take a particular direction may not be the same in all groups and hence only general guidelines can be framed to understand these, rather than suggesting very specific tools or strategies to either predict or control them. For example, the way events will develop in a group of children will be different from that in a group of adult rural women, or a group of workers in an industry. Similarly, the processes in a recreation group will be different from the events or behaviour of different actors in a task-oriented group.

The cultural context is also a factor in influencing the processes in groups. For example, the group processes in Indian rural villages in case of a self-help group of women will be different from a self-help group of women in New York. The women in India are far more dependent on the worker and are likely to develop group norms in conformity with existing social norms. The development of emotional content is far smoother and faster than on the task front. Decision-making is obviously not very problematic as it is worker directed, and how far it will be democratic depends on the workers skill to enlist a wider participation. Sub-groups also develop on anticipated lines, particularly if it is a mixed caste group. Cohesiveness of the group depends on how spontaneously the women join the group or how well they understand and identify with the purpose of the group. If these conditions are absent the cohesiveness will be missing, in the sense that the members would not be according a high priority to group or its relationships. In short, the behaviour of individuals and the group as a whole is what we need to understand by way of group processes.

An important issue in understanding what is happening or is likely to happen in a group, is to keep the actual nature of group in mind. For example, the behaviour, relationships and decision-making in a natural group such as family or peer group will be different from that of formed groups.

Let us first see what types of processes different authors identify, which are happening in the groups. Douglas identified the following and put them in a tabular form:

Classification of Group Processes

Category 1	Basic	Interaction
Category 2	Structural	Group development, social structure, sub-group formation
Category 3	Locomotive	Decision-making
Category 4	Molar	Formation of norms, standards and values, Development of cohesion, development of group pressure, development of climate.

Ridgeway (1983), who wrote about the dynamics of small groups listed the following group processes in chapter on fundamental processes in small groups. She identified:

1. Communication
2. Cohesiveness
3. Group development
4. Conformity
5. Deviance
6. Social control
7. Status differentiation
8. Leadership
9. Group culture

Toseland and Rivas (2001) felt that the forces that result from the interaction of group members are often referred to as group processes or group dynamics. The authors admit that despite several attempts to classify group dynamics, or in other words, identify group processes, none has proved very satisfactory. They, however, identified four processes they thought are vital in understanding the group functioning:

1. Communication and interaction patterns
2. Group cohesion
3. Social control
4. Group culture

It is interesting to note that the early authors of group work like Trecker (1948), Konopka (1963) and Helen Northen (1969), do not talk about group processes. Konopka has a chapter in her book where she discusses theories of group process and generally talks about how the group begins and finally reaches its goal or goals. The more focused approach of the later authors is a reflection of professional growth in the area of group work. The basic idea is to look at the functioning of either natural groups or groups which are specifically formed to identify specific processes. These need to be understood in order to understand the total group functioning. In other words, what happens in a group and how far it can be influenced to conform to some specific trends and final outcomes, depends on a worker's understanding of what is happening in a group.

Looking at the processes discussed above, one can see some remarkable similarities, which is an indicator of the universality of what happens in groups. However, as we indicated earlier, the analysis of these events can be different. The interaction is the starting point, and facilitating this process is another process, which is communication. Both of these should either lead to cohesion or conflict or deviance and hence another process emerges, which is group control. In wanting to give a direction to the group either worker or members themselves take initiative and thus the process of leadership emerges and decision-making gets underway. Gradually, members begin to understand and value some behaviours and norming begins. The group starts showing progress and a definite movement towards goals, better understanding among members, a division of roles and responsibility, which is an indicator of structuring within group, and also group development, is noticeable. It is obvious that the processes are interrelated and the overall functioning of the group will depend to a great extent on the way these processes unfold in the group. The subsequent search then begins to develop an analysis of why interaction resulted in cohesiveness or conflict. A discussion of these will help in developing professional competence of handling groups, as it will help a worker to know what to expect and how to deal with the situations.

The key events likely to happen in a variety of ways in the group will be:

1. Interaction
2. Communication
3. Cohesion
4. Conflict
5. Structuring
6. Leadership
7. Decision-making
8. Norming and group culture
9. Social control
10. Group Development

Interaction

People join groups for a variety of purposes. These may be to accomplish tasks that cannot be carried out individually since a group would be more cost efficient to meet socio-emotional needs etc. Interaction in a group is a natural phenomenon. The interaction begins as people come face to face in a situation. The interaction process is fluid and undergoes frequent changes that may lead to either conflict or cohesion in a group. Communication, both verbal and non verbal, facilitates interaction. In working with group, a central concern is to learn about the patterns of interactions, how widespread they are, are they making the group or breaking the group. Interaction focused around a central goal makes a good beginning, and indicates that the group is in the process of evolving. On the other hand, when several themes are being discussed among two or three people, the interaction is diffused. This is indicative of lack of focus and order in the group. In Indian conditions, this is a normal occurrence. The focus is achieved through the initiative of either the worker or leader or both.

Interactions can be person or issue focused. Person focused interactions may suggest interpersonal conflict. In such cases members are either carrying out their frustrations or are contesting for power spaces in the group. One person dominated interactions will result in concentration of power in the group. Such a person will determine its purpose and direction and will influence the participation of other members. S/he will even impose restrictions on interaction of members among themselves. In such situations the interaction will be focused but could be autocratic. This domination can however be questioned or contested by members. A central concern is to identify conditions that facilitate domination, even though it may be helpful for achievement of the group goals. The nature of power, its location, and the individual styles of leadership, along with the nature of the group and its objective, will influence the nature of interactions. Interaction can become emotionally charged. These patterns reflect the way members are looking at themselves and others in the group. Other factors influencing interaction are:

- The nature of relationship among group members
- The degree of homogeneity among group members
- The nature of group goals
- The nature of leadership
- The size of the group

The general sociological understanding is that larger the size of a group, lesser is the interaction among its members. Interactions in smaller groups tend to be easier and more intimate. Social work groups formed for a variety of reasons are kept small to monitor the interactions more closely. In larger groups the presence of a large number of people and the greater diversity among members put a strain on interactions. The largeness of the group in a way increases both the physical and psychological space among members thus influencing the interactions.

The relationships among members or the 'emotional bond' between them to use the term employed by Toseland and Rivas (2001), is an important influence on the interactions in a group. The relationships influence the communication and interaction of members and vice versa. Relationships get distorted in absence of proper communication. Similarly, a negative relationship between members can distort the communication. Positive relationships lead to an increase in interaction among members, whereas negative relationships tend to restrict communication and interaction. Negative relations in a group will dilute the focus of the group. The members' energy will be wasted on winning individual battles. Social status of members influences, the interaction pattern in a group. These trends are often visible in a panchayat (local body) meeting, and also in any discussion in a group in the community. The women and Dalit members interact according to their social status, as also the common peasant, while the elite dominate. Age hierarchies are also observed in group interactions in rural areas. Social or formal status of members influence interactions in formal groups too.

The degree of social distance among members poses a large strain on members, as is evident from the example given above. Balgopal (1980) termed it as 'allogenic conflict' and argued that it needs to be given due attention in group work. He suggested that the usual assumptions in group work that a successful group leads to greater cohesion and new behaviours, may not be entirely true in conditions of allogenic conflict. In treatment groups where the safe environment is a key, controlling the heterogeneity among members is a vital factor in group intervention. Mahler (1969), for example, suggested that if a member is incapable of interacting with other members, s/he should be left out of the group. This indicates how important the compatibility factor is in treatment of groups.

The nature of group and its purpose – growth orientation, task orientation or treatment – influences the interaction. Task orientation dilutes the focus on emotional content of the group and makes interaction more routine and structured. In task oriented groups the agenda has specific issues and the group functions within a prescribed time frame to resolve all the issues. In treatment and growth orientation more openness in interaction is encouraged. The focus is on monitoring the emotional aspects of the interaction among members. The group has to allow sufficient time for members to unburden their personal problems. Interaction in formal groups is different from interaction in informal groups, because in formal groups the power is formally located and the role structure and hierarchy is also formally determined, providing a definite direction to interactions in the group. Leadership is perhaps the key variable in understanding interaction. A democratic leader in a formal group laying emphasis on emotional content can make interactions as informal as in an informal group without losing focus on the task or goals. At the same time, an autocratic leader may dominate the interactions in all types of groups, whether formal or informal, large or small.

The isolate or low key participation is indicative of an interaction pattern, where some members are keeping a low profile, remaining at the periphery of the affairs of the group. People may adopt this pattern of interaction for different reasons. A common interpretation is, lack of interest, and/or lack of adequate skills to interact, but the reasons could be varied. People may remain silent during a group session since they feel the others will not be able to understand their intervention, which is a case of extreme differences. At other times they remain a spectator because they are unsure about the intentions and commitment of others, indicating poor bonding.

The sub-group is another interaction pattern inevitable in some groups, where people are likely to find interpersonal attraction more striking in a small number of people within the group. Gender bonding, regional, religious and caste affiliations, and interest bonding, commonly induce sub-group bonding. The patterns of interactions can be like the following figures:

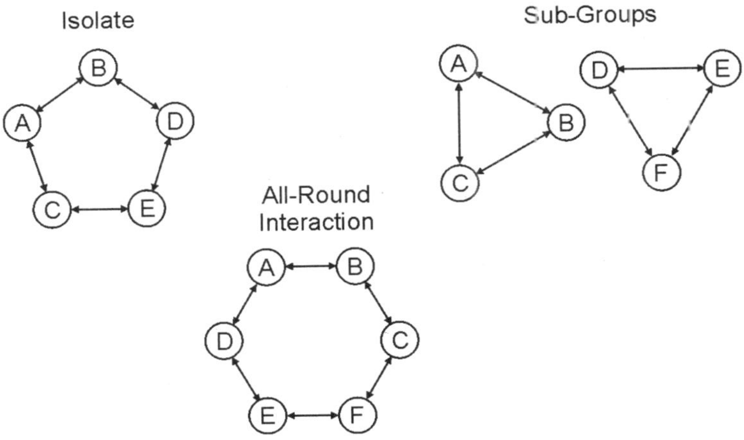

Some of the possible ways of improving interactions in groups can be:

- Controlling the size
- Reducing social distance
- Developing effective leadership

- Clarifying group goals
- Creating and maintaining trust
- Explaining interaction patterns in the group
- Dealing with fears and resistances
- Making internal feelings explicit

Communication

Communication is one of the vital aspects of interaction among the group members. The quality of communication makes an immediate impact on the group. A negative communication style can hurt feelings and may induce disinterest among members. A positive communication pattern on the other hand may relax members. Communication alerts group members to differences in needs, behaviours, abilities and opinions. Communication itself thus starts laying the foundation for the division of labour and status hierarchy and friendships in the group. A skilful communicator is an asset for the group. There are possibilities of distortions occurring in the communication process. The communication process needs monitoring to ensure smooth flow of information among members to create a healthy environment in the group. Misunderstandings can occur and unintended consequences of communications are quite common. Gaps in communication can also cause a number of problems in various facets of group functioning. The formal groups pay a lot of attention to work out the details of their communication system. However, informal groups are not very particular in developing an adequate system of communication. They rely more on informal arrangements of communicating with each other. For example, in case of informal groups of women, the date and time of meetings or other arrangements would simply be conveyed orally and no written records are generally kept. Minutes of the sessions are seldom recorded and even records of responsibilities allocated are seldom maintained. This needs to be streamlined as per the requirements of the group.

Communication is the vehicle for both standardization and differentiation in groups. The nature of the communication pattern also helps in the evolution of the social structure in groups. It is important for the worker to understand that communication channels take time to develop in a group. In the initial stage, the communication channels are fairly widespread and informal. After a period of mutual assessment, based on skills, needs and interdependence, the communication pattern gets stabilized. Definite patterns of communication start emerging, reflecting sub-group formation. The process in group development enters a new phase, influencing the functioning of the group. The new formations, so long as they remain functional and focused on group goals, allowing wider participation, are not contested. However, formations with exclusive tendencies generate conflicts in the group. The group cohesion and group development flow is restricted. The members feel that they are being left out and neglected. The group is a reflection of the wider social context of its location.

Groups that are formed by a worker tend to be worker oriented with the worker controlling all communications. With a few exceptions generally the members come from a lower socio-economic background. In such groups the capacity of members to communicate effectively in a group is limited. It is necessary to undertake a process of capacity building to improve the communication skill of the members.

Cohesiveness

Group cohesiveness can be simply defined as willingness on the part of all members to stay on in the group. Interaction in the group, as suggested earlier, can have the following consequences. People either like each other and enjoy being in the group or they stop participating in the group activities. Groups not engaging in any definite activity or providing members any material benefits, but still able to hold them together, reflects high bonding and cohesiveness. The cohesiveness in adolescent groups, adults group in *chaupals* (common meeting place) in rural areas, and Sunday groups of neighbours or women's gossip groups are some examples of cohesiveness. These groups are spontaneous and natural, and members join them on their own. The nature of cohesiveness found in groups formed by workers, work groups and families, is different. The cohesiveness in these groups is more fluid and the situation changes with different events and activities. The internal and external environment of these groups is dynamic. It, therefore, influences many aspects of groups functioning including its cohesiveness status. Cohesiveness, however, is not simply a factor of members liking each other or interpersonal interaction, as it is called. People want to stay on in a group because of a variety of reasons, the group potential for meeting needs, material or non-material being an important one. People stay on in a group despite competing with each other and having negative feelings towards each other. The reasons may be to get a loan, to gain recognition in the community, or to have security as member of the group. In such cases, where members wish to stay on in a group, the power of the group over the members increases. The group is able to influence members' behaviour. Goal attainment improves as members put extra efforts to achieve group goals. Creation of such environment in the group to increase the commitment of members is central to group work. This is by no means easy as no strategy is likely to be universally applicable. The factors which help in making groups cohesive are: group norms and culture; group goals; a caring leader; a non-threatening group environment; and a greater degree of homogeneity among members. The sources of cohesiveness identified by Ridgeway (1983) are: special norms and practices designed to build members, commitment to the group; interpersonal attraction; social structure and leadership style; interdependence among group members; group's relationship with its outside environment; attraction of group goals and activities, and so on.

Group Conflict

When human beings come together to work, play or carry out any other activity, conflict is inevitable. To quote Rousseau, "man becomes wicked in the company of fellow human beings". Differences among members in a group will occur in resolution of issues such as to select the group goals, to have control over resources, to decide strategies to pursue the goals, to create a group structure and in distribution of power. In a self-help group of women, the concept of empowerment, financial contributions, loan disbursement and selection of office bearers are all issues likely to generate differences. Group conflict may present a wide variety, such as between individual members, between member/s and group, between a member and the leader/worker, between members and leader/worker and between sub groups. The reasons for conflict may differ, depending on the context. The nature of conflict in a treatment group, for example, will be different from that in a task group. Many authors agree that conflict will generally start in the middle, working or performing stage (see Toseland and Rivas, 2001). In a treatment group, conflict is generally between members. The reasons may be miscommunication, which results in lack of trust and defensive behaviour. Inadequacy to deal with diversity is a common cause of conflict in all kinds of groups. Similarly, exclusionary practices are a potential source of conflict in groups beside ego clashes. Heated exchanges, silence, negative feedback, personal remarks directed against individuals, attacking the integrity of individuals, are all symptoms indicative of conflict in a group.

Some potential sources of group conflict can be summarized as follows:

- Miscommunication
- Ideological differences
- Rigidity of group structure
- Cultural differences
- Inability to accept diversity
- Location of power
- Leadership styles
- Group goals not addressing individual needs of a sizeable section of group
- Plurality of options
- Outside environment
- Lack of clear group norms
- Paucity of resources
- Greater heterogeneity among members

The capacity to deal with a conflict varies among members and the inability to deal with conflict effectively produces stress. It is normal for people therefore to avoid conflict. A confrontation means to take a stand on any issue, or more simply, to express your views even though they are different from that of the majority or the leader. The result is pressure to conform. The stress is higher for the person taking a stand in a group in absence of support from others. Things become complicated when the majority is on the other side or become neutral. In groups with power of reward and punishment the stress is higher than in other situations. There is a difference between a hostile confrontation and a caring confrontation. A caring confrontation is to help members make an honest assessment of themselves or to speak more about their own reactions rather than talking about others (Corey and Corey, 2006). A negative confrontation is designed to hurt others. Often people are not sure why they are doing what they are doing. It is obvious that confrontations in groups have the potential to affect the development of the group and the individual members.

Strategies to Deal with Conflict

The sources of conflict identified above are also indicative of how we can reduce conflicts in a group. For example, lack of clear norms can create conflict in a group. The solution is to develop group norms, as they help in providing clarity to members about how various issues should be handled in a group. Location of power refers to structure of authority in a group. In social work groups, the golden principle of providing equal opportunity to all members to participate in decision-making, is helpful in resolving conflict related with location of power. Some of the steps to reduce conflict in a group are as follows:

- The first step in dealing with any type of conflict is to acknowledge the fact that there is a conflict.
- Make the members face the situation openly and help them to express their views.
- Make an objective analysis of the views expressed in a participatory manner. In particular try to separate the issues from the persons.
- Summarize all the facts and present them in an orderly manner before the group.
- Seek professional expertise if necessary in resolving complex issues.
- The worker/leader must remain neutral in all conflicts.
- Help the group to develop clear norms for taking decisions, interacting with each other and in expressing their views, etc.
- Help the members to accept differences, particularly to accept cultural diversity.
- Reduce heterogeneity in the group, if need be advise members to take appropriate decisions regarding the membership.
- A discussion on structuring will help in further highlighting some of the issues relating with conflict and how to deal with them.

Structuring

Group structure refers to the allocation of roles and status to members in a group. The process of structuring begins with group functioning. Tuckman (1963) suggested that storming is reflective of members contesting for spaces in a group. The concept of social distance is a useful one to understand the respective positions of members in a group. Age, social and economic status of members, their intellectual abilities including technical and professional competence, gender, etc., are all important factors in determining their status in the group relationships and power sharing. The process of assessment of members is continuously on in a group. The structuring based on an ongoing process of objective assessment of members' contribution to group, helps in reducing conflict in groups and promotes confidence among group members. In groups with a higher degree of social distance among members, this is not generally the case. Members are happy to assume a more passive approach on account of social distance, thereby reducing the possibility of conflict. They may in fact feel shy of accepting power positions. Both people from lower castes and women tend to exhibit such a tendency, particularly in groups which are heterogeneous in character.

All members in a group are neither similar in skills or experience they possess of functioning in a group, nor do they have similar motivations for joining the group. Members' status rank can generally be deciphered from three behavioural patterns: their participation level in group activities, the valuation of their participation by the group, and the degree of their dependence on group. The structuring in groups emerge as they get focused on achieving the group goals and avoiding competing claims and conflicts of sharing the rewards of group achievement (Ridgeway, 1983). French and Raven (1968) has identified the following types of power that help in enhancing an individual's status in a group:

Connection power: relations with influential people in society and ability to get any work done.

Expert power: expertise in any area which can facilitate the group's task.

Information power: information about different matters which is needed by others and that can facilitate group's work.

Legitimate power: a position of authority.

Reference power: liked and admired by many persons in the group.

Reward power: to be able to reward social or other benefits to people.

Coercive power: ability to punish, harm or deny access to resources.

Ridgeway (1983), on the other hand, noted that there are four classes of attributes and behaviour that enhance status of individual members in small groups. They are: external characteristics, objective competence, dominance behaviour, and socio-emotional behaviour.

External characteristics refer to characteristics of an individual that provide him/her high status in the society in general, for example high caste or high economic position, occupations rated higher in society, etc. Even natural characteristics such as height, age, attractive personality and so on, that are generally valued in society, also adds to one's status in a group.

The objective competence is having special skills to contribute to the group development or task accomplishment.

Dominance behaviours refer to assertive behaviour, being able to contest a point, win an argument and so on.

Socio-emotional behaviour is like the referent power suggested by French and Raven. In addition members perceived motivation towards the group. The group too accords a higher status to members who display greater attachment to group interests rather than self-interest.

It is important to ensure that the group structure is not very skewed and affords due opportunities to all. There are various ways in which group leaders, workers or group facilitators can ensure this, but the structure of the group can be modified only up to a point. This is the reason why a certain degree of compatibility is to be ensured from the beginning to facilitate the development of a group. It is also necessary to ensure a certain degree of other orientation among all members, to ensure smooth functioning of a group. Democratic norms are difficult to adhere to in practice, particularly in groups with a high achievement orientation.

Group Decision-Making

Group decision-making is the process of arriving at a decision where more than two individuals are involved. It is important to understand the process of decision-making to analyze the functioning of a group. Decision-making patterns can be analysed to predict group functioning. Groups follow some broad models of decision-making. These are described below (see Lahiti, 1996):

Group performance is largely dependent upon the nature of decision-making processes that a particular group uses. Decisions not based on facts reduce the chances of the success of a group. Similarly, the decisions to cater to the interests of a section of the group, would lead to conflicts in groups. In all groups, numerous decisions have to be made ranging from group goals to place of meeting. These decisions involve resources (i.e., in the form of time and energy) of the members. The quality of decisions and the process determine the outcome of the group. Group environment plays a major role in the decisions and the processes involved in making these. Social capital facilitates the group decision-making process. The choice of decision-making model may not be a conscious choice of members, but may be a forced one. The following models are followed by groups in decision-making:

The Rational Model

The rational model is based upon an economic view of decision-making. It is grounded in goals/objectives, alternatives, consequences and optimality. The model assumes that complete information regarding the decision to be made is available and one correct conception of a problem or decision to be made can be determined. The model further assumes that the decision-makers are capable of assessing the advantages and disadvantages of any alternatives with goals and objectives in mind. They then evaluate the consequences of selecting or not selecting each alternative. The alternative that provides the maximum utility (i.e., the optimal choice) will be selected.

The most salient advantage of the rational model is that it utilizes a logical, sequential approach. Decisions are made deductively by determining the goals or objectives to be obtained, evaluating the potential alternatives based on the information at hand, and choosing the optimal alternative. In other words, the model is simple and intuitive in nature.

The rational model does possess a salient disadvantage. The model assumes that there are no intrinsic biases to the decision-making process (Lyles and Thomas, 1988).

The Political Model

The political model suggests that decision-makers bring their own interests and conceptions of the problem at hand to the table in the decision-making process. In contrast to the preceding model, the individuals involved do not accomplish the decision task through rational choice with regard to objectives. The decision-makers are motivated by, and act on their own needs and perceptions. This process involves a cycle of bargaining among the decision-makers, for each to get a perspective to be selected. More specifically, this process involves each decision-maker trying to sway other members within the group to adopt his or her viewpoint to influence the decision (Allison, 1971; Cheshire and Feroz, 1989; Lyles and Thomas, 1988; Schneider, Shawver and Martin, 1993).

The political model does not believe in making full information available or focussing on the optimal viewpoint like that of the rational model (Lyles and Thomas, 1988). In fact, information is often withheld in order to better manoeuvre a given perspective. Since information is often withheld and subsequently incomplete, the optimal viewpoint is not a key aspect of this model.

Personal interests and biases are common among members and inevitably influence their behaviour. An acknowledgement of the fact will help in anticipating the potential problems and conflicts and in devising ways to deal with issues. Conflict can be minimized by swaying powerful people to support a viewpoint. Once the powerful people support the perspective, other group members usually fall in line (Lahiti, 1996). It may however not lead to the best solution. The nature of bargaining and manoeuvring (e.g., withholding information and applying social pressure) can produce effects that are long-lasting and detrimental.

The Process Model

The process model of decision-making is more structured. In this model, decisions are made based upon standard operating procedures or pre-established guidelines within the group. Actions and behaviours occur in accordance with these procedures or guidelines (Cheshire and Feroz, 1989; Allison, 1971).

Conformity is an integral part of the process model since it is the means by which doubt or disagreement is dealt with during the decision-making. If decision-makers are uncertain as to the potential effectiveness or the results of a decision, they conform to the pre-established standard. In this case, conformity merely relates to the fact that the reasoning for the decision is based upon pre-determined guidelines (Cheshire and Feroz, 1989).

An assessment of capacity of members will help in ensuring participation. The decision-making process reflects the nature of power and its use or misuse in groups. In India, the decision-making in groups presents, a wide variety. The groups in formal settings are influenced by formal leaders and follow the rational or process model rather than the political model. Others formed by workers follow the rational or political rather than the process model.

Leadership in Groups

Leaders facilitate the group functioning. A leaderless group faces problems in maintaining order and focus in group functioning. All groups, either formally or informally, elect or select leaders to facilitate the functioning of the group. The development of leadership significantly affects the development of the group. As pointed out earlier, the effectiveness of a group is measured on two main indicators, i.e., the emotional environment and the task orientation. It has been suggested that some leaders are more task-oriented whereas others are more happy to keep the team together. In groups different leaders provide inputs to enhance the goal attainment. The leadership has the potential to harm the group. Unfocussed leadership results in wastage and delays goal attainment. In such groups the functioning would be full of tension and conflicts and the very continuance of the group would be threatened.

Social scientists do not believe that leaders are born. The leadership qualities among members can emerge from different sources. As Lewin suggested, leadership is a function of interaction in a group. The composition of members, their socio-economic background, skills and experiences, their prior relationships and affiliations, and their achievement orientation, play a part in the process of emergence of leadership in groups. Although there is no consensus on who is a good leader but a person who is able to provide a solution to a group problem and is willing to invest individual resources in handling group problems is valued. There are different perspectives on group problems and how they should be solved. Robert Terry (2001) identified six theoretical perspectives of leadership: leadership as power; organizational leadership; trait theory; situational leadership; visionary leadership; and ethical leadership.

Some theories identify power as the central factor in leadership and then go on to identify different kinds of power. French and Raven (1960), for example, identified five types of power, referred to earlier in the text. In referent power, a person is seen as having the capacity to provide guidance to others in their problems. Such a person emerges as a leader, as the effectiveness of his guidance is tested by people over a period of time and is found effective. Expert power refers to a person seen as having specific expertise in an area, such as financial matters, legal matters, health issues, etc. Legitimate power is the power that comes to a person through his or her official position. Reward power refers to persons capable of offering rewards such as teachers, managers, parents and people having any type of authority, etc., and finally, coercive power refers to people who can harm others including physically strong people. All people who are able to help you in getting things done are seen as people having power. In groups such people are respected or feared by others and may emerge as having a different or higher status than other members in the group, thus turning them into leaders or special persons.

At the initial phase of a group a process of members assuming leadership roles in the group will commence. The theories outlining types and sources help the worker to understand the type of leadership developing in the group and how it will affect a group. In India, caste, class and gender factors influence the leadership roles in a group. In case of a group of children, these factors are less relevant. The play skills or physical characteristics and fitness play a crucial role in determining leadership roles.

Norming and Group Culture

Norms are shared expectations and beliefs about appropriate ways of behaviour. Violations invoke social sanctions. Norms serve as guideline for acceptable behaviour. All groups establish norms and belief systems. Some are borrowed from the social context of the group, while others are part of the cultural background of members. Norms about acceptable dress, observing due courtesies, greeting forms and acceptable communication styles are present in all groups and are followed. Norms about status, roles, strategies and processes for goal attainment evolve as a group develops. They serve to structure the functioning of a group and reduce the necessity of a continuous negotiation of the rules governing the functioning of group (Whitaker, 1995). Norms serve the political function of distributing power as well. This is helpful for the smooth functioning of a group. Norms restricting the well-being of members can also emerge, such as a belief in complete obedience to hierarchy, and gender biases. The functioning of groups often undergo a chaotic phase to induce changes. Accepting things as they are help in accomplishing smooth functioning of a group, but lead to stagnation and poor outcomes both on the emotional level and task level. There is often a tendency on the part of a powerful subgroup to force compliance from others by citing the need for maintaining harmony in group. The phenomenon is known as groupthink (see Irving Janis, 1982). Janis identified this as pressure on people to agree, not to disagree. Butler (1987) discovered a similar tendency among members to maintain status quo, which he referred to as cooperating with others consciously or pre-consciously to reinforce prevailing attitudes, values, behaviours, or norms. The goal of such behaviour by member or members in a group is self-protection. This can strangulate democratic functioning of the group and may lead to alienation and frustration among members in the long run. To maintain dynamism groups can continuously undertake self review of norms and other aspects of functioning as well.

In groups people often revise their understanding of issues to accommodate other view points. However, individuals differ in terms of accommodation of differences in order to achieve conformity in group. The norming becomes a problem when there is a wide range of beliefs and commitment to various values. Norms regarding sharing of power and resources are difficult areas to cover. Procedural norms covering all areas of group activity are helpful in promoting clarity about how to handle situations in a group. It also helps in providing a guideline for individual members to accept different roles and tasks. Some roles are more demanding than others in the group, and so often there are not many takers for these roles. Similarly, some roles have greater power. It is difficult to evolve norms of role allocation acceptable to all.

Group Culture

The philosophical or cultural norms define the group culture. Group culture defines the entire lifestyle or worldview of a group. Some groups would tend to be more formal, for example, a group formed to achieve a specific task in a commercial or government organization, while a group formed to work with children or women by an NGO would be more informal in its culture. Groups evolve their own symbols and philosophy as they settle down and relationships among members assume a more permanent status. In India, as compared to the west, the emphasis in working with groups is to encourage more long-term relationships in groups. Some groups may stay together for years though members may change. In such cases group culture is more distinctive and leaves a more permanent mark on the behaviour of members. In short-term groups the culture accommodates more differences among group members by allowing them more freedom. This is not possible in long-term groups, where conformity to group norms is greater, for maintaining lasting partnerships.

Social Control

Order is a prerequisite for the functioning of a social unit such as a group. As noted earlier, groups develop norms to regulate members. However, deviance is common. A system of control is inevitably developed to enforce compliance. Firstly, there are written codes of conducts. These are formal rules of conduct and the violation of these evokes a specific penalty. The other kind of rules are not coded, but made well known to members through a process of socialization. These are known as social norms, code of ethics or etiquettes. The process of socialization imprints the consequences of violation on the psyche to make it effective. The group social control in India follows a similar pattern. Only formal groups such as commercial organizations or formal associations develop written rules, while other groups follow a more informal approach. Physical punishment or public ridicule are quite common among groups of children for enforcing control, while cold shouldering a person or excommunicating is common among adult groups of all kinds for enforcing control. Some positive ways are confronting the persons and persuading them to conform to group norms. Groups also use reward system by acknowledging compliance by elevating status. Leaders and workers both play a role in developing control mechanisms in groups. Professional groups experiment with different ways of controlling.

Group Development

Group development refers to the process of progress groups achieve over a period of time. Two specific indicators are: (a) the members feeling settled and happy in the group; and (b) progress the group is making in achieving its objectives. Regular meetings of the group, a wider interaction among the members, a free flowing conversation, laughter, general spirit of cooperation and accommodation, are signs of a positive environment in a group, reflecting a clear sign of group development. A growing activity schedule, increase in savings, creating an asset such as a water source, a cooperative business enterprise, achieving a change in the members coping mechanism, and mental health status, are all signs of group development as well. On the other hand, growing conflicts and tensions, decline in membership, decline in number of meetings held, declining schedule of activity, and boredom and stagnation among members, are signs of lack of group development.

Stages of Group Development

A stage of development or growth in a group is defined here as a specific level of achievement in task accomplishment and emotional integration of members in a group. The stages of group development helps the worker to monitor what is happening in a group. There is no unanimity among authors in conceptualizing stages of development. The area of research on group development is known as temporal environments of small group. Most studies in the area focus on therapy, training, or self-analytic groups (see Lacoursiere, 1980; Moreland and Levine, 1988). The result of these studies are difficult to evaluate because they involve qualitative analyses of a few groups (often only one). These studies are not always clear about such issues as the number of stages through which groups develop, the behaviours exhibited by group members during those stages, the rate at which group development occurs, and so on. Most theorists argue that group development is a recapitulation of the childhood experiences of individual group members. Other factors that might affect group development, such as: (a) the beliefs and expectations that current members share about their group (Long 1984); (b) the entry of new members or the departure of old ones (Moreland Levine, 1983); and (c) changes in the group's physical or social environment (Gersick, 1988), are rarely acknowledged. It is important to remember, however, that every group operates at some developmental level and that its level of development is bound to change. Several studies (e.g. Schriesheim, 1980) show that the effectiveness of a leader's style depends on the developmental level. However, there is considerable agreement about what trends develop in a group, despite the different views taken by authors about the sequencing of these, as we shall see later. It should be clear, too, that the group development stages must be viewed as an organic, unified whole, rather than as a series of separate parts. All of the various parts interact and influence each other, and each must be thought of in relation to the other.

It is obvious that like individuals, groups of individuals too would not remain the same over any period of time. Yet, by the term 'group development' what is referred to is not how the individuals in a group are changing but how the relationships in a group are changing. They either improve or they deteriorate. People may start looking at each other as friends or as enemies. It is also possible that certain relationships may get more stabilized and as a result the development of the group may altogether stop or remain stagnant for long periods. But experience tells us that the intensity of both positive and negative relationships continue to change. The scope of relationships also continually increases or decreases. Hence, generally relationships change rather than remain totally stagnant. Generally, the well-known models of group development identify a linear arrangement of development stages, where one stage is expected to precede or follow the other stage, such as the forming, storming, norming, performing and adjourning, provided by Tuckman (1963). But now some models of group development do depict a cyclical arrangement of stages, whereby conceding the possibility of development stages to be seen more as an ongoing process rather than the neat arrangement of one following the other, for a variety of reasons. Theory of cyclical stages talks about repetition of stages throughout the lifecycle of a group. The relationships among members and with worker are the main focus in group development. As Konopka (1963) noted, the relationship of the members to each other are rather complex and full of meaning and possibilities. They are never static. They change in time and in relation to specific situations and events in the life span of a group.

There are some groups which settle down very quickly and are able to achieve their goals without much disruptions. Other groups might take a long time in resolving their differences, and never settle down to concentrate on a task or goal. We will discuss the reasons and analyze the events in a more focused manner later when we discuss working with different client groups (also see the discussion on cohesion and conflict). The developments in group would be influenced by a number of factors which are universally applicable. We have a number of studies identifying reasons for why some groups are more successful in achieving both the emotional stability and the task, while others face more problems at both levels. To begin with, group structure, communication and interaction, leadership, group goals, and group norms and culture, have been identified as important factors in the process of the development of a group.

Bales (1950) was perhaps the first person to study and describe the stages of group development. In his studies of groups he noted that the first thing that people in a group do is to familiarize themselves with other people in the group and explore the possibilities that the group has to offer to them. He called it *orientation stage*. Bales went on to suggest that next thing members do is to analyse the information gathered and reach some conclusions about what kind of members are there, whether they are trustworthy, helpful and cooperative and how they look at the other members, what the group therefore can offer to the members, its activities and programmes and so on. The members may review their relationship with others in general and form their conclusions based on their experiences so far. He termed this stage as *evaluation stage*. The analysis or the evaluation of members about the people, programmes and benefits would then lead to a decision about their participation and action in the group. The group would also reach a stage of relationship among members where they can take collective decisions about matters in the group. Bales termed it as the stage of *decision-making*. Northen (1969), in her description of group development, seems to follow Bales, though she termed the middle phase as *exploring and testing* which leads to a stage which she terms as *problem-solving* and finally *termination*. The focus of group development is on relationships in the group. The use of the term *problem-solving* in the context of relationship is confusing. Northen, in her later work in collaboration with Rosella Kurland (2001), suggested that "following the initial stage, there is a period of exploration of relationships and uncertainty about power". The process of evaluation as suggested by

The Stages of Group Development

Bales (1950)	*Tuckman (1963)*	*Klein (1972)*	*Trecker (1972)*	*Garland, Jones and Kolodny (1976)*	*Northen and Kurland (2001)*
Orientation	Forming	Orientation	Beginning	Pre affiliation	Inclusion-Orientation
Evaluation	Storming	Resistance	Emergence of Group Feeling	Power and Control	Uncertainty-exploration
Decision-Making	Norming	Negotiation	Development of Bond	Intimacy	
	Performing	Intimacy	Strong Group	Differentiation	Mutuality and Goal Achievement
	Adjourning	Termination	Decline in Group Feeling	Separation	Separation-Termination
			Ending		

Bales (op. cit.) and *resistance and negotiation* as suggested by Klein (1972), appears to be a good description of the next stage after the initial stage of orientation. Klien's description is confirmed by Tuckman's use of the term *storming* to refer to the process of exploration and negotiation in a group. Northen and Kurland go on to suggest that, "as uncertainty is resolved" and members come to terms with their relationship with each other and the worker, they are able to work together and thus enter the next stage of group development. The worker at this stage would do well to focus on the emotional issues arising out of the relationships. Garland, Jones and Kolondy (1976) term the second stage as *power and control* and suggest that the main task of worker is to deal with matters arising out of settling the power issues in the group. If these issues are not adequately dealt with, it can lead to hostility towards each other in the group as also towards the worker. Power issues are however never adequately settled. The negotiations reached at a time can change with the passage of time and also as the group confronts new situations both internally and externally. The experiences suggest that a policy of role allocations based on merit and role equalization, whereby all contributions by members are given due recognition, certainly helps. With every member developing a sense of self-respect and partnership in group, power issues are likely to settle down well.

5

Principles of Group Work

In social work practice it is customary to evolve principles of working with different units of people such as individual, groups and communities. The tradition of doing so started as social work perceived the situations as a practice reality, and from the perspective of a practitioner they thought it more pragmatic to talk about do's and don'ts of practice rather than suggesting a theoretical framework. Social science theory is difficult to formulate on account of a number of reasons. In early twentieth century particularly, the social science theory was in a nascent stage. It is not surprising, therefore, to find that many authors writing about group work, devoted considerable time in outlining the principles of working with groups. For example, in 1935, Kingman and Sidman delineated the following principles of group work in the context of youth work in USA. They however added before they went on detailing these principles, that knowledge of the basic principles of group work in itself cannot prepare one to be a professionally skilled group worker. This acknowledges the need for other forms of knowledge and a theoretical understanding, to become a professional. The other interesting thing, which a review of principles developed by different authors indicates, is the similarity in conceptualizing the important areas of focus for a practitioner. For example, Kingman and Sidman outline the following areas:

1. The aim of group work is to develop people, not programmes, and the activities carried on are merely a means by which this aim may be accomplished.
2. The programme should be developed in accordance with interests of the group.

3. Discovering interests is a continuous process.
4. The programme of activities should be flexible and dynamic.
5. There should be a maximum of initiation and participation by the group itself.
6. Length of an activity should be determined by needs and response.
7. Finding new outlets for undesirable behaviour.
8. Adjusting the individual to the group.
9. Conflicts may result in constructive experiences.
10. The type of organization depends on the status of the group.
11. Group Leadership is an opportunity and a challenge.

It is clear from the way Kingman and Sidman define the purpose and process of working with groups, that the group work was seen as an input to develop the individual members and inculcate an ideology of democracy. The principles are a good reflection of common sense understanding of what will work and what will not, described in a very uncomplicated manner. What should, however, be noted is that the context was the development of adolescent and children through the group work. Kingman and Sidman were not considering the use of this process in other group work contexts though they raised some very important issues such as development of individuals and resolving conflicts in groups. More insights on the part of worker are needed to handle these issues, which we will be discussing in detail later. Kingman and Sidman had that in mind when they noted that mere knowledge of these principles may not be enough for acquiring professional expertise of working with groups effectively.

In 1948, Harleigh B. Trecker in his famous book, *Social Group Work: Principles and Practice,* devoted a full chapter to the principles of group work practice. The principles identified by him are:

1. The principle of planned group formation
2. The principle of specific objectives
3. The principle of purposeful worker group relationship
4. The principle of continuous individualization
5. The principle of guided group interaction
6. The principle of democratic group self determination
7. The principle of flexible functional organization
8. The principle of progressive programme experiences

9. The principle of resource utilization
10. The principle of evaluation

He concluded at the end of the chapter by saying that the principles of group work will change as group work develops in future and as new insights are discovered. The principles of group work suggested by Trecker seem to be based on the experience gained from workers in practice and are looking at working with group as a set of specific activities such as planning, guiding, decision-making, resource utilization and evaluation, etc. It is not envisaging any special understanding of, for example, therapies or management expertise, etc. It does not evoke any theory of group functioning which may be considered necessary for working with groups. The basic purpose seems to be a learning experience for members in groups. The worker is expected to be a well intentioned and civilized person groomed in democratic ideology. This is much the same conceptualization as was earlier done by Kingman and Sidman. The other striking similarity is that group work is basically seen as an activity with children and adolescents. The principle of progressive programme experiences in particular seems to suggest that. My own thinking as a student was so much influenced by these books, that for a long time I considered group work as an activity of primarily working with children and youth. In 1962 Ruby Pernell presented a paper 'Identifying and Teaching the Skill Component of Social Group Work'. She talked about activity areas evolved by Etta Saloshin (1954) in her doctoral dissertation, such as accepting, relating, decision-making, limiting behaviour, guiding discussion, alleviating tension, conflict and fear, interpreting, observing and evaluating, and finally planning. Konopka (1963), in her book, discusses all these prior to attempting to formulate the principles of group work such as:

1. Individualization in the group
2. Individualization of groups
3. Acceptance of members
4. Relationship between worker and group members
5. Developing cooperative relationship between group members
6. Modifying the group process
7. Encouraging participation on the part of members
8. Enabling members to participate in problem-solving
9. Satisfactory resolution of conflicts
10. Providing new experiences in groups of relationships

11. Diagnostic assessment of members
12. Purposeful use of programme
13. Ongoing evaluation
14. Disciplined use of self by group worker

The way Konopka (1963) looks at group work is different from the earlier conceptualizations. The principles of diagnostic evaluation and ongoing evaluation are new concepts signifying the therapeutic possibilities in the use of group. This also enhances the scope of group work practice by opening up the possibility of adult clients.

By now certain key activities which the worker should pay attention to in group work, and which are commonly found in the description of various authors (see Douglas, 1979; Hartford, 1972; Helen, 1969) are becoming clear, These are: paying attention to individuals in the groups besides group goals or objectives, anticipating and attending to a wide variety of groups rather than expecting all groups to be similar, solving problems and resolving conflicts in groups, making good use of programme and relationships in the groups, and continuous evaluation of every aspect of group dynamics including self evaluation. However, the context of group work remains development of members, and the democratic functioning and equal opportunity principles are kept intact. The concept of task orientation perhaps at this stage had not emerged. Many schools in India and other developing countries in Asia, I believe, continue to see group work as an activity of working with children and youth. Despite the recent popularity of self-help groups in Asia, the classroom teaching contents are not emphasizing these or treatment goals. The task orientation is gradually figuring to some extent but the overall activities identified earlier seem to be the focus of classroom discussions.

In the west, on the other hand, and in particular in USA, the use of group for treatment purposes is becoming more popular and a variety of professionals are using it. These professionals are also contributing more to recent literature on use of groups for various purposes. For example, Sharry (2001) in his book *Solution Focused Group Work*, talks about the following principles of group work:

Principles of Solution Focused Group Work (SFGW)

1. *Focusing on change and possibilities:* This principle suggests that it is important to become more specific about changes sought and also creating a hope and expectation that these could be achieved.

2. *Creating goals and preferred futures:* The expectations to be turned into goals and problems to be considered as past and solutions as the preferred future.
3. *Building on strengths, skills and resources*
4. *Looking for what's right and what's working:* Looking at the positive side of the picture.
5. *Being respectfully curious:* to discover the strengths of the clients or members rather than their problems.
6. *Creating cooperation and collaboration*
7. *Using humour and creativity*

Sharry is emphasizing self-help and a shift from problem focus to solutions. The approach differs from traditional therapies in the sense that its focus is not on problem or its causes but on preferred futures and goals. Stated simply, the trend is away from explanation, problems and pathology and towards solutions, competence and capabilities (O'Hanlon and Weiner-Davies, 2003). He argues that the group has a unique power of its own and that it could be used for a variety of purposes. Sharry has argued for a short-term more focused use of group work, basically for therapeutic purposes only, which he terms as solution focused brief therapy. He claims that it has been successfully used with such client groups as children and adolescents in schools, relaxation groups in mental health day care centres, patients in psychiatric hospitals, parenting groups, perpetrators of domestic violence, anger management groups and parent training programmes. The basic characteristics of the brief group interventions are described as:

- Clear, specific goals which can be achieved within a given time frame
- Establishing group cohesion
- Focus on recent issues and problems
- Client homogeneity
- Focus on interpersonal rather than intra-personal issues
- Therapist acts positively and influences directly the dynamics in group

He specifically identifies the therapeutic factors of group work and compares them with those identified by Yalom (1995).

SFGW Sharry (2002)	*Yalom (1995)*
Group Support	Universality (sense of not being alone) Group cohesiveness Catharsis
Group learning	Imparting of information Interpersonal learning Developing socializing attitudes Imitative behaviour Corrective recapitulation of the primary family group
Group Optimism	Instillation of hope
Opportunity to help others	Altruism
Group empowerment	–
–	Existential factors

Sharry therefore presents a very different perspective of group work. In fact, he emphasizes on the therapeutic power of the group (we shall discus in detail the process and content in the chapter on process). The difference in activity focus can be clearly seen here since the objective and context are different than the earlier conceptualizations of group work. In 2003, Wendy Bunston et al., described the following principles of group work in an article published in the *Australian Journal of Social Work* as principles of growth enhancing practices in group work:

1. Creating safety
2. Commitment to supervision
3. Use of self and others
4. Attunement to process
5. Holding the individual in mind with in the group
6. Recognizing the importance of play
7. Surrendering your territory

They described the basic function of group work as creating growth-oriented therapeutic encounters for children, young people and adults. Bunston is a social worker with a family therapy background and Paul Leyden is a psychiatric nurse Tara Pavlidis, the other co-author is a social worker in a Community Group Programme. Their emphasis is also on therapeutic goals in group work as at least two of the authors come from a therapy background. In fact, one of the reasons why some of us who taught group work did not emphasize on therapeutic goals was that we thought this would require the use of therapies where the competence level of social workers is rather limited. It is interesting to note that people from therapy background emphasize supervision as a principle. This is a good indicator of the need to recheck our strategies and methods, while we are attempting behaviour change. Bunston et al. emphasize the use of self as also of others and significantly argue about team work rather than seeking exclusive claim to working with groups, as they rightly suggests surrendering territory or becoming flexible, in working with a team consisting of different professionals. Other principles are same as that conceptualized by others.

Toseland and Rivas (2001) however used a different approach in identifying principles of group work. They identified the following elements or components of group, which they felt will provide a foundation for a good understanding of group dynamics. They evolved principles of practice under each separately.

Communication and Interaction Patterns

The principles discussed under this category are:

- Principle of communication: indicating that communication is inevitable in group and worker's role is to encourage effective communication in the group.
- Communication patterns can be modified.
- Communications are motivated.
- Message perception is selective.
- Messages may be distorted.
- Feedback is helpful.
- Open group centred communication is to be preferred.

Group Cohesion

Principles of practice relating to cohesion suggest:

- Open interaction promotes cohesiveness
- Achievement of group goals makes the group more attractive for members
- Non-competitive, intra-group relationships, supporting members, perception and point of views, promotes cohesion
- Competitive inter-group relationships help to define group identity and purpose

- A manageable size of group help in promoting cohesion
- Need fulfilment of members help in promoting cohesion
- Understanding and addressing expectations of members help to promote cohesion
- Rewards, resources, status or prestige, not available to members outside the group, increase the prestige of the group

Social Control

- The principles of practice of social control suggest that social control helps in stabilizing the group processes.
- Group structure helps in maintaining social control.
- Overemphasizing the structure can strangulate the members, participation and may prove counterproductive.
- Members would follow social control dynamics that are helpful in promoting cohesion.
- Members would observe social control norms if group goals are attractive and meaningful.
- Social control would work if the members continue to value their membership.
- Rewards and sanctions are helpful in maintaining social control.

Group Culture

The principles of group culture suggest that:

- Group culture emerges through an intermixing of values
- The values of the agency, community and society at large also influence the group culture
- Individual members' and workers' stereotypes can conflict with group culture
- Value conflicts can affect cohesion in the group
- Group culture can influence members' values
- Group culture supporting members' socio emotional needs stabilizes the group

Group Development

The principles relating to group development suggests that stages of development are more predictable in case of groups with a closed membership.

- In groups where the membership is open the turnover of members affects the development of the group.
- The beginning stage in groups is generally explorative.
- It is followed by norm development, role testing and status assessment and differences.
- Differences may lead to conflict.
- The groups manage to resolve conflict and experience task accomplishment.
- Finally, the task is finished.
- Groups may experience strong emotions about ending.

Toseland and Rivas (2001) thus identify five significant areas of group work practice and try to deal with each of these by suggesting what would help in achieving better results in practice.

The principles of group work are, therefore, trying to provide a set of guidelines for the workers to achieve the desired professional competence. These guidelines are based partly on the experiences gained from working with groups and partly from the general understanding of social sciences, though sources are not cited explicitly. These principles are contextual as well, as they depend to a great extent on what the client group is and what specific objectives are being pursued as well. It is difficult, therefore, to arrive at a general guideline, which could be universally applied in all group work practice situations. However, one can make an attempt to work out generic principles of group work practice, which will apply in all situations and then try to work out specific principles of different situations. This task can become more systematic if we try to identify activities or situations, which may require a specific response from the worker, for example formation of a group. Now, we know that this is not a general situation as many of us work with already formed groups. Also, the formation process in case of a treatment group will be different from that of a recreation group or self-help group for savings and credits only. Yet, the specific method to be followed in forming a group in different contexts needs to be discussed. We shall deal with it, therefore, in the list of specific principles. In working with groups we are bound to face individuals and groups. How do we deal with them in a professional manner? There appears to be a general agreement among scholars that both are important and individual needs and group goals both have to be addressed. This situation will arise in all groups with whom an intervention is planned. So. we will include it in the area of generic principles. All group work interventions will commence by setting up their objectives and doing some advance planning to achieve these. Similarly, the creation of a safe environment is the key, which helps in accomplishing the desired objectives in all groups. This therefore can be another area to develop guidelines for standardizing our professional responses. Assessing the ongoing process or processes in groups is another activity, which workers will have to address in all groups. Finally, bringing to a close any intervention will have to be addressed in all situations. The generic principles of group work practice as we conceive these are:

1. Principle of dual objectives of addressing individual and group goals
2. Principle of planning
3. Principle of creating a safe environment
4. Principle of monitoring and assessing the group processes
5. Principle of termination

Having worked out the general principles, let us identify the specific situations which will be faced by workers in different settings. We have referred earlier to the situation of forming a group. Some groups will face conflicts and hence the worker must be prepared to address the situation in a professional manner. Some scholars have felt that individual workers may need supervision. What are the situations where the worker may feel the need for consultation or help from other professionals and how should s/he manage such situations professionally is another area we should pay some attention to. So, the specific principles of group work practice would be:

- Principle of group formation
- Principle of conflict resolution in groups
- Principle of supervision

We shall now discus in detail what we mean by these principles. As we argued earlier, the sources for drawing the practice rules or guidelines, as we can call them, have been the experiences of working with clients in general, social science theories, and general observations of human behaviour in everyday life.

Principle of Dual Objectives of Individual and Group Goals

This understanding has been with the scholars right from the beginning of group work practice that individual needs are important and have to be at the centre of group work practice. As Kingman and Sidman (1935) have noted, the purpose is to develop people. At the same time, they have noted that group is important since the development of members is achieved through the group. This principle is to be kept in view to achieve a higher level of professional competence since situations often arise where a group is having a number of programmes going but they are being designed and controlled by only a few people. They are not addressing the needs of all members. As we have argued elsewhere, the principle of equality may or may not be a part of the group norms, but democratic functioning is a central concern. This is a theoretical insight gained from social sciences that if every member of a small group does not get a chance to participate in the activities of the group and he or she has a feeling that his or her needs are not being addressed, the member is likely to become disoriented and may even discontinue the membership. This situation has also the potential of giving rise to conflicts and destroying the cohesion of the group.

The principle also clearly indicates that all individuals are different. Though a certain degree of homogeneity is sought, depending on the nature of group goals, the group processes have to be flexible enough to accommodate the human diversity. The individual needs and problems, even if different from others, will have to be taken note of and addressed. One may even use the principle of reference, if the individual needs cannot be met in the group. This applies to all groups since each group will have differences. The worker should be able to take note of these differences and accordingly modify the strategies of handling group processes. For example, all groups cannot progress at the same pace. The worker shall, therefore, allow adequate time for such groups to develop at their own pace. The participatory methods of defining needs and developing an understanding free of our own biases are helpful in looking at cultural differences and consequently different group cultures and their functioning. While paying attention to individual needs, the focus should remain on group goals. Balancing group goals and individual needs requires careful planning.

Principle of Planning

The hallmark of a professional approach is that things are meticulously planned and executed in an efficient manner, leaving little to chance. A group can only become an efficient medium of helping if it is planned carefully with the objectives of the sponsoring agency, and the needs of the prospective members along with their current capacity to participate in the group activities kept in focus. Each little detail has to be worked out in advance. Clarity about the specific goals the worker has in mind, or the benefits that the worker is hoping to provide to members of the group, is important. How and when this is to be shared with the members also needs to be planned in order to avoid over expectations or disagreements among members about what to expect. Doing it right in the beginning is helpful for subsequent smooth sailing of the group. It is also important to plan the overall model the group is expected to follow, i.e., is it a recreational group, growth oriented or a treatment group. Accordingly, the procedure for recruitment of members, the size, frequency of the meetings, and number of workers, etc., would be determined. Another thing to be planned is the time frame and the actual time and place of each group session.

Advance planning is needed for identifying the programmes and activities and the resources needed to carry them out. A policy of generating resources and its utilization would have to be planned as well. Trecker (1948) has given a very useful insight about programme planning by simply defining it as moving from simple to complex. All groups take time to settle down and gradually start functioning at a normal pace. The group picks up momentum or starts stagnating, depending on the programme planning. If activities are meeting the members' needs, it will keep the interest of members alive and focused. The worker, therefore, keeps the activities simple and less strenuous in the beginning and gradually increases the complexity of tasks, as the members settle down. In treatment groups, till the members are sure of the environment in terms of the safety or support it offers, they are not likely to become open and start sharing their problems and experimenting in the group.

The decision about membership is important, i.e., whether it will be open or closed. This decision should be part of the planning. As suggested earlier, a decision about the degree of heterogeneity or homogeneity is to be taken along with group structure. Similarly, how many workers will be involved with the group should be planned in advance.

Planning should also be done about what mechanisms and sources would be used for monitoring the progress of the group. However, despite the planning, the worker should be prepared to deal with the numerous things that are bound to arise when the group starts meeting. This is known as planning for contingencies or unforeseen situations. A professional worker is however able to anticipate many such things and therefore is mentally prepared to handle all situations.

Principle of Creating a Safe Environment

The success of group work to a great extent depends on creating a safe environment. This has many requirements beginning with the establishment of a positive relationship between worker and members and among members as well, as was indicated by Trecker, Konopka and a number of other scholars. Acceptance of each other by the members is a major requirement for creating a safe environment. Bunston et al. put it succinctly when they noted that growth occurs when safety is in place, which means that members are emotionally, physically, socially and spiritually safe. This situation allows them to express themselves freely. The degree and nature of safety again depends on the client group and the group goals. For example, recreation groups would provide a different kind of safety than the treatment groups. It simply means that members will not hurt each other. Therefore, the worker should take appropriate steps to ensure this. It is also important to remember that things change and the acceptance may turn into rejection and positive relationships may become negative. The development of group norms and a group culture, as also mechanisms of social control, as pointed out by Toseland and Rivas (2001), are efforts in the direction of maintaining a safe environment.

The cohesiveness in the group is what members enjoy most, i.e., when they feel that they belong to the group. At times the feeling can become so powerful that it can even dilute the individual's self-confidence to survive on its own without the group. Naturally, when the cohesiveness is at its peak, a member will not like to leave the group. This feeling helps in making group attractive for them and it makes them to do things or make compromises to stay on. But this also can make them very particular about who is a member and who is not. Anyone who they think is working against the group interest, would be conceived as an enemy and it can arouse passions to protect the group. A strong indicator of cohesiveness is where each member has full confidence in the rest of the members and therefore the member feels fully secure in the company of others. This confidence in others ensures the acceptance of others and the acceptance of the structure. That is, the members accept both the role and status accorded to them as just. They, in a sense, stop competing against each other, since they feel that the others are an extension of their own self, and they fully enjoy the achievements of others. There are many factors, which may contribute to the cohesiveness of the group but as Trecker (1948) noted, the acceptance of each other is the most important. The ability to associate depends on the degree to which people share norms and values and are able to subordinate individual interests to those of larger groups. Out of these shared values comes trust..... (Kay, 2002). Even if there is one member the other members cannot trust, the cohesiveness will be affected. Festinger (1950), through his studies, indicated that interpersonal attractions play a vital role and thus can help in measuring the cohesiveness. Schutz (1958) developed a test to measure how suited the people were, in interacting with others. He identified three dimensions of personality: personalness, power and assertiveness. On the basis of a test of these qualities, a profile can be constructed for each individual. However, important as it may seem, other factors should be taken into account to understand cohesiveness. Feldman (1968) identified three characteristics of groups to keep them working together. He also considers interpersonal attraction as one which he terms as interpersonal integration. The second factor he identifies is the nature and effectiveness of group structure, which leads to structural-functional integration. The third factor he identifies is the shared beliefs and rules and practices leading to normative integration. This is in line with what we pointed out earlier while referring to the way Toseland and Rivas (2001) look at group culture, norms and communication patterns that affect group processes.

Communication is an important factor in influencing the group processes. It has been observed that misunderstandings can occur among the best of relationships and unless these are monitored and rectified it could destroy any relationship. The major causes of misunderstanding are lack of communication, distortions in communication or misinterpretations of communication. A safe environment can be defined as a location where people feel free to communicate.

They are never misunderstood and never ridiculed or punished for what they communicate. The important point to remember is the fluidity of these happenings and shifts and changes taking place in a group, yet not to discount the fact that a certain stabilization can occur and may last for a long time. We may have to return to a discussion on cohesiveness later, during the discussion of actual process of working with groups. We have already discussed the importance of creating a safe environment and what it means to the members (see the factors affecting social development chapter 4 and social science research on groups chapter 2).

Principle of Monitoring and Assessment of Group Processes

This principle is to remind workers that constant monitoring is essential to keep track of happenings in a group. The purpose of monitoring is to get periodic information in order to arrive at an understanding of the progress or stagnation in the group. We are deliberately not using the term diagnosis, as this creates an impression that group work is treatment or problem-oriented. Assessment is a more general term applicable in all settings. We need information about how each individual is feeling and assessing the group activities, whether the participation has increased or decreased, is the group becoming cohesive or otherwise, and is the communication effective or restrictive. And above all is the structure facilitating or obstructing the group functioning. We need to have a good idea about the time frame of the group activities. Are things happening as per schedule or are they lagging behind? For example, we wanted that the group should get over the formation stage in such and such time, is that happening as per schedule? This is only one aspect of our inquiry the second aspect is why we are lagging behind. How will the worker assess whether the formation stage is over or not or how the members are feeling? Another important aspect of monitoring is, how the workers are sharing the work load among themselves or if there is only one worker, a self-assessment of the worker's role.

There are several ways to collect information about these matters:

Members are a potential source for getting information. We can ask the members to give us a self-assessment report about any aspect or all aspects of the group functioning for a particular time period. The members can also give a self assessed report of their own feelings and involvement in the group. They can even be asked to assess other members' behaviour in the group.

Worker's observation: Worker's observations are another potential source of assessment related information. Worker's observation about the functioning of the group and the analysis of members' behaviour is a very vital source for assessment. The assessment details and focus will be different in case of each group as the group goals would vary. In case of treatment oriented groups, standard tests can be used for assessment of progress or changes. Treatment groups where behaviour modification is the objective, would go in for more details about a member's family, work and general background assessment as well. This would require more information. Some of these details can be collected from the members as a routine requirement to join the group. Some of this could be collected during the pre-session interviews with members, if any are planned in specific contexts.

In India, for example, group is being used as medium for empowerment of women. In such a context, an assessment of family environment or work environment and the general cultural milieu would always be helpful in assessing the changes and the members' behaviour (for more details, see the chapter on process and stages of group development). Programmes or activities designed to assess the members or the group cohesiveness can also be carried out in the group (Toseland and Rivas, 2001).

Principle of Termination

The process of group intervention, like all other professional interventions, is designed with a time schedule in mind. It has to come to an end, although the group in some cases may continue to exist and function. This makes it necessary for us to give some thought to this aspect of group intervention. It is obvious that it should not happen in an abrupt manner. In other words, it should be planned as suggested in the principle of planning. The decision about termination can only be made after a careful assessment of facts. There are two aspects of termination. One is regarding the services of the worker to the group. The second is regarding the continuation of the group as such. The decision to continue the group should be that of the members since even if the worker may express the inability to continue with the group, the members can continue the group. The worker would facilitate the decision and prepare the members to carry it out in a planned manner.

In India, there are many groups which are planned as a long-term group, where the termination refers to the termination of facilitation by the worker only. The group is expected to carry on functioning as an independent institution or unit. The self-help groups of different varieties fall in this category. Even many other groups such as play groups or youth groups in community, or elderly groups in day care centres or in the community, can go on for as long as the members feel the need for it. In all such cases, the termination phase is preparing to leave on the part of worker or workers as the case may be. The worker needs to ensure that:

- Members wish to continue the group;
- Rules or norms regarding the functioning of the group have been developed with full participation of members;
- Some members have been trained to take over the leadership role;
- A system of periodic rotation of group leadership is also in place;
- More importantly, the worker has made an assessment of the group development and feels that the group has reached a level of stabilization or degree of cohesiveness to survive on its own.

There are many instances where groups end abruptly or there is a general drop in membership. This can happen on account of a number of reasons such as in the case of children and youth play groups, school exams are likely to commence shortly, or the interest of the members is wearing out. Even change of weather at times may lead to a drop in membership. In case of group of rural women, their domestic work patterns or field related activity pattern may have changed. It can also happen on account of their participation being opposed by some segment including husbands or village elders. All these instances need to be probed. They reflect that the planning was not as professional as we expected it to be. A professional worker will know details like when generally the children are likely to be busy with school examinations and so on. S/he should anticipate changes in work, at home or in the agriculture fields or any where and s/he should also monitor the level of interest in the programme and activities. These precautions and planning will help in avoiding unplanned changes and abrupt endings.

The abrupt endings also happen when conflicts in groups get out of hand, or the group is not making any further progress. In business terminology it may be said to be the case where benefits are too insignificant compared to costs of participation. The situation could be when nobody wants to go to a meeting, where nothing comes out of it and one has to invest a lot of time and other resources to attend it. A professional worker would know how to keep ahead of these difficulties by applying her mind to take care of many of these problems during the process of working with group.

Specific Principles

- Principle of group formation
- Principle of conflict resolution in groups
- Principle of supervision

We now turn our attention to specific situations that we shall encounter and discuss principles, which will help in dealing with these situations.

Principle of Group Formation

In India, workers generally have to form the groups. There are few situations where they work with groups already functioning in a hospital, school, and residential institution or in a community. This may be for a variety of reasons: (a) some groups stop functioning as soon as the worker withdraws from the group; (b) the practice of handing over the group to another worker is not very common; and (c) many organizations do not use the concept of supervision in working with groups.

The process of formation of group will vary with the group objectives and type. A task-oriented group, for example, a recreation group of children, youth or elderly, or awareness generation groups such as legal aid groups of women can be formed without worrying too much about the degree of compatibility among members, or the socio-economic differences, etc. In contrast, a treatment group or a social action group formation would require pre-group formation sessions with individual prospective members. Group formation in India is a difficult task since in many cases, the worker has to convince the clients to join a group. The women in slums and in rural areas are one such client group. Both alcohol addicts and drug addicts show a disinclination to join groups. This makes it necessary for a worker to plan a strategy for dealing with the resistance of potential members.

The group formation requires a clear understanding on the part of the worker about the objectives, the client population, the location of the group, frequency of group meetings, duration of meetings, and so on. In India, people are generally not aware about the worker or the sponsoring organization or their motives for such activities. Therefore, the group formation begins with meeting the prospective members and some others, who will not be joining the group, but who will still play a major part in the formation and subsequent functioning of the group, for example, parents of children and adolescents, husbands, village elders, leaders in the community and so on. The worker needs to realize that group formation or the participation of members in groups will affect a number of people and they will react in different ways to the group and its activities.

The interpersonal compatibility should be given due attention, particularly in areas, where caste, religious or regional factors can create difficulties. Age and gender are important considerations in formation of the group. Because of the difficulties mentioned, formation of groups, may take a longer time in some situations and hence the worker should plan accordingly.

Principle of Conflict Resolution in Group

Some groups work smoothly while others face problems on account of group conflict. Conflict resolution in India is more serious problem in natural groups such as family, work groups and community groups. However, in formed groups such as a self-help group, conflict can occur quite frequently. Play groups of children and adolescents frequently witness conflicts but they are different in nature as generally they involve ego clashes or a clash of preferences about games or other activities. Conflict in adult groups is more complicated, particularly where it involves distribution of benefits and power.

The nature of conflict will vary in different groups, particularly in different client groups. Task groups will have different problems than treatment groups and growth-oriented groups. Secondly, the conflict will not disappear by itself, hence ignoring it will not help. The situation will have to be faced and resolved. Often ignoring conflict gives wrong messages, particularly the leadership may be seen as weak and not willing to take unpleasant decisions. Members may feel that others are not willing to face the truth. Sometimes unpleasant facts should be suppressed to keep everyone happy or to keep the group going. One also needs to differentiate between minor differences and major differences. The normal procedure for conflict resolution is to:

- Accept and inform the members about the nature of conflict.
- Try to create a supportive climate for the resolution of conflict.
- Look for an explanation about the possible reasons for conflict.
- Try to ascertain facts about the situation, for example what is the central issue.
- Help others to express their opinion.
- Use decision-making techniques of exploring options and choosing the best by involving every one, by logically ruling out the options which are not functional.
- Help members to look at facts objectively rather than subjectively.
- Leader or facilitator has to remain neutral and help the conflicting parties to realize that resolving the conflict will help everyone.

However, experience tells us that some conflicts are difficult to resolve and require more radical measures including restructuring of the group. The leader or facilitator may persuade the conflicting individuals or sub-groups to move on but that does not mean that the differences have been resolved.

The conflicts can basically be categorized as personal conflicts, technically referred to as affective, or ideological (cognitive) conflicts. Personal conflicts are rooted in interpersonal relations, where the personality traits are causing the problem. In ideological conflicts, the basic differences arise on account of different set of values and methods of working for achieving goals. Ideological differences can also provide the basis for subsequent personal clashes or interpersonal differences. For example, some members feel that the group structure should be horizontal, whereas others feel that it should be vertical. Generally, the basis of conflict is a greater degree of heterogeneity among members or among influential members.

All groups are a reflection of the society at large. Members bring their social attitudes with them. A recent typology of individuals focuses upon self and others orientation. A self orientation refers to a person trying to maximize his or her return from every interaction or trying to control everything. The others orientation refers to a person who is more concerned about how an action would affect others or how one could help others. Obviously, most individuals carry a balance of the two, but with significant differences. Conflict generally arises when two extremes come together and the differences are so severe that they are unable to make even a functional adjustment. Other causes of interpersonal conflict are biases and prejudices, and above all, lack of experience to interact with people different from us. Capacity building of members to accept diversity can reduce conflict.

Principle of Supervision

It is good to remember that we are all human and despite our training, professionalism and competence, we can make mistakes by ignoring or misinterpreting facts while analyzing or handling situations. During the T-group experiments, Grace Coyle (1947) noted that the groups were not handled properly by the trainers as they gave her the impression that they knew all the answers. It is, therefore, always important to have some kind of arrangements in place to review the working of professionals, particularly while handling situations stressful for both clients and workers.

Treatment groups need more careful handling. Supervision would greatly help in reducing the risks involved in misinterpretations or lack of sensitivity to client's feelings and needs. The proper handling of team relationships, flexibility to transcend boundaries and develop cooperative attitudes of sharing and transparency, also enlarge the scope for a more client-friendly competent practice.

6

Process of Working with Groups

Several authors have studied the process of working with a group. There is no agreement on the stages of the process, as different authors use different terminologies to describe these. The number of stages also differ among the authors. Some begin from a pre group formation stage to the termination or the final stage, whereas others may start with the beginning stage or the first phase and go on to the ending stage. However, there is a kind of uniformity in conceptualizing that the process should commence from planning and it should have a termination stage or phase, where the worker withdraws from an active involvement. Planning activities as Toseland and Rivas (2001) term it, are generally discussed by all. Planning about forming the group includes making a decision about the target population, the broad objectives to be pursued, the resource availability, and other factors relevant in India. The *planning stage* is followed by the *orientation stage* by some, whereas others simply term it as the *beginning stage*. The next stage is the *middle stage* or *working stage* where the group has started functioning and is trying to accomplish some goals. At this stage it is generally found essential by different authors to undertake an assessment or evaluation of what is happening in the group. Some, therefore, term it as *evaluation stage* (see Toseland and Rivas, 2001). In the termination phase in India, after a careful analysis, a decision to continue or terminate is taken. The worker helps the group to make the necessary preparation and accordingly plans to provide inputs for continuation or termination. This stage is termed as the *termination stage,* though it may not mean termination of the group in India. It refers to the end of a worker's full-time direct involvement with a group. The process of working with a group is outlined below for a clear understanding of the process.

Pre-Group Planning

The workers have to work hard to form a group in India. In many cases they are not sure of the objectives. They have no idea where to begin and what they are supposed to do. According to the stages referred to earlier in the process of forming a group, the pre-group planning stage refers to contacting potential members individually or in small groups to share with them the idea of forming a group. The process significantly differs from that followed by workers in the western countries. Groups in India are initially conceived by an organization or a welfare agency, as people themselves generally do not take such initiatives. Both the voluntary organizations and the government organizations have found working with groups a useful strategy for accomplishing a number of objectives. The worker in India therefore, has to carry the idea of forming a group for an already identified objective to the people. S/he has to educate the potential members about the needs or issues that the group will address and how it is likely to benefit them. The worker generally meets the potential members for the first time and many members have little or no experience of working in such groups. The formation stage thus will require careful planning. There are two sets of plan that a worker must prepare. The first part of the planning concerns how the formation of the group will be accomplished, and second, what issues will arise once the group gets going and how these will be dealt with.

Many a time the general assumption is that the members' need is well known, for example the economic need or the recreation need of children and youth. Yet, when the idea of forming a group is shared, not many members show interest. The answer lies in the fact that children do not feel the need for an organized group to play. Things in their day-to-day life have never been organized and the very idea of any form of organization is a very unknown phenomenon to many. It therefore, takes a long time to make them accept the idea. It is very important for the formation of a group that a worker presents the idea of forming a group to potential members in a very clear and unambiguous manner. Secondly, workers must clearly indicate how the group activities will meet a specific felt need of the members. The importance of following a participatory approach cannot be overemphasized. The worker should carefully analyze the need of the clients as her own perceptions may not be the same as those of the clients themselves. If there is a wide gap between the members' perception of what the group can deliver and that of the worker the group development will be slow or the group will not take off. The worker should contact the members individually and in groups to discuss the idea and purpose of group formation. At this stage the worker should also be on guard about forcing the idea on members. It is possible that the clients may, in order to please the worker, readily agree to join the group but do not turn up later. The worker should be patient and undertake activities/decisions to show results in the first few sessions of group formation, to arouse the interest of members.

In treatment or support groups meant for adults facing a problem, the pre group planning would address the importance of sharing the problem with persons facing similar problems and how it would lead to greater clarity on the part of members to deal with the problem. The worker should aim at, as Yalom (1995) suggested, in preparing the members for creating an alliance. Provide members some idea how a group therapy session works, and how inter-personal relationship can be enhanced through the use of group therapy. The worker can also help them to understand some basic rules of participation in group therapy sessions. The members can also be briefed about the duration of the group, its size, nature, meeting place, etc.

The planning for forming a group in particular should focus on the following details:

Composition of the Group

The nature of membership depends on the purpose of the group and its goals. Client or target population is an important factor in determining the composition of the group. Corey and Corey (2006) recommend a homogenous membership in treatment oriented groups. In task oriented groups, some element of diversity is helpful in getting better expertise level to address the task.

Collect details about the members on the following points:

- The socio-economic background of members
- Geographical location – urban, rural, tribal
- Client group – children, women, etc.

- Earlier experience of group participation
- Reasons for joining the group
- Individual need assessment

Take a decision about the composition of the group after analyzing the details. Collecting information about these issues will help the worker to get organized in carrying out the work. It will give her some idea about the background of the potential members. Need assessment helps in assessing the response of the potential members. Take a careful look at group goals and make sure that they are in conformity with the needs of the members.

Size of the Group

A decision about the size of the group should be made keeping the purpose of the group and the needs of members in mind. In Indian situations at times the worker faces the dilemma of how to say no to persons eager to join the group since s/he is not in a position to accommodate them due to shortage of resources. Large groups however, offer more ideas, skills and resources (Douglas, 1979). Treatment groups are kept small to enable the worker to focus on each member, while self-help groups are allowed to have more members to make them financially viable. The decision about the size depends on several factors including the experience of worker and the age group of the clients.

Nature of the Group Membership

The issue of membership, whether to keep it closed or open, is decided in accordance with the purpose and duration of the group. In growth oriented groups it is better to allow new members to join if there are vacancies, in order to enrich the experience of the group and to extend an opportunity to a larger number of people. Treatment groups find it difficult to admit new members as this can change the existing environment of the group.

Duration of the Group

The decision about the duration is taken considering the purpose, experience, and capacity of the members to achieve the goal in a given time frame. Many group workers try to form groups with a long-term perspective. The general idea is to make the group self sustaining, so that it can function independently. A good example is self-help groups of all types in India. Treatment oriented groups are short term groups with a specific time frame to achieve specific objectives. Support groups like women's group or street children's group, are also generally long-term groups. The duration of the group can be changed depending upon the progress made by the group, such as a certain level of cohesion and the decision of the members to continue on their own.

Frequency of Group Meetings

The frequency of group meetings are to be fixed depending upon the purpose, convenience of members, the workers' own work load, etc. As such there is no fixed formula to decide the issue. For example, recreation groups of children meet more frequently, support groups once a week or once in 15 days, and self-help groups or saving groups weekly or once a month and so on. Frequency of treatment groups is decided more in accordance with the needs of the members.

Place of Meeting

A place of group meeting has also to be decided in accordance with the convenience of the members and the facilities in terms of space and other resources needed for group activities. Frequent change of venue of meeting is known to cause difficulties and should be avoided. Members' consent about the place of meeting is helpful as at times the place of meeting could severely affect the participation.

The Beginning Stage

Facilitate Members' Familiarity with the Group

In the first meeting of the group the worker can undertake simple activities which help the members to get to know each other. Forming pairs to tell each other about yourself and chatting for two three minutes about things in general can often provide members enough time to start talking with each other. In case the group members are from the same community and they already know each other, the worker simply introduces the sponsoring agency and him/her self if s/he has already not done so in the pre formation stage. S/he can then go on to elaborate on the purpose of forming the group.

One of the main objectives is to deal with the anxiety of members, i.e., their feelings of uncertainty about the group experience, how to handle themselves in the group, the fear of rejection and so on. Building trust in the group and its activities is a major issue to be handled at the beginning stage.

Making members familiar with some of the basic rules of participation in group activities can be explained at this stage. Different procedures can be followed in developing the rules. Some workers prefer to do their homework by preparing a set of model rules and they share these with the members. Other workers provide more freedom to members to work out their own rules and procedures. A third method, in case of agency sponsored groups, is to make members aware about the agency requirements or norms for membership in the group. Some points to be included in formulating procedures about participation in groups are: attendance, regularity and punctuality about time, eating and drinking, use of alcohol and other drugs, use of offensive language, confidentiality, respecting the diversity and differences, socializing with members outside the group, parents' permission in case of minor children, democratic nature of group functioning and general courtesies to be observed towards each other.

Procedures about any evaluation and feedback to be provided by members should also be explained at this stage. The clarity about procedures helps to lessen anxiety among members.

Clarify the Purpose

The worker may have talked about the purpose during the pre formation stage but it is still advisable to restate the purpose in more detail. For example, in case of self-help groups, the purpose could be savings and income generation. The various steps involved in achieving the purpose, the role the members are expected to play, the role the leader/s are expected to play, the role the worker is expected to play, and so on, should be spelled out in detail. Using the same example of self-help group the worker should explain to members that they are expected to discuss and decide the rate of monthly saving to be made by each member. They have to identify a person who will collect the sum and maintain an account and so on. The leader's role will be to convene meetings and to remind and motivate people to attend the meetings and contribute their share in time, etc. The worker will help them to find a financial institution nearby, help them open an account and train them in carrying out their respective roles.

The expectations of members from the group and workers, expectation from members and leaders should be clearly described, so that every member understands the role they are expected to play in meeting their own and allowing others to meet their needs. It will also help members to have greater clarity to tone down their individual expectations and be more realistic about what the group can offer.

Set Goals

In setting goals we need to be specific in identifying a goal. Sometimes, there is a tendency to use broad categories, for example to eliminate child labour or generate awareness about HIV/AIDS or women empowerment, etc.

The goals should specify the actual outputs which are likely to be achieved as a result of the intervention process or inputs. For example, if child labour is to be eliminated as a result of the group intervention planned by forming groups of working children and mothers, the goals should be stated as:

- To develop trust among members to work together;
- To form a fund through savings to free them from indebtedness; and
- To train members to start small enterprises, etc., and so on.

In case of treatment groups the goals should be stated as:

- To help members to learn to trust others;
- To help members to express themselves; and
- To help members to learn new coping strategies to deal with stress, and so on.

In case of growth oriented groups of children:

- To help members learn about their strong points;
- To help them learn about their weaknesses; and
- To help them learn how others feel about them, and so on.

Clarity about goals can motivate members and help them to assess their progress periodically. The goals should be explained to members along with the role they are expected to play. Members should be encouraged to clarify their doubts right in the beginning.

Set the Routine

Once these matters have been dealt with, the group should decide about the frequency, place and time of meeting, etc. Other matters regarding developing norms can be taken up at this time. The activities calendar for the group should be prepared as also the procedure for supervision and management in the group. The purpose is to set a routine pattern for the group to follow. The most important task at this time is to keep motivating the members by clarifying their doubts about the feasibility of group objectives and the specific benefits that are likely to be there for every member. The group activities will show some ups and downs in the beginning, but are likely to become routine and stable once the members become sure of what they are doing. It will be a slow process in many cases because of the members' socio-economic background in India. Some capacity-building activities, literacy classes, skill building such as communication exercises, can also help in setting the momentum in the group.

Distribute Roles and Responsibilities

The structuring of group can commence as soon as members have settled down and have started showing interest in the group. Everyone should be made clear as to what is expected of her/him in the group. Members having expertise to contribute to group task or goal achievement, or those capable of bringing about emotional integration of members, should be encouraged to use their expertise to provide a direction to the group process. Members should also be helped by the worker to learn how to carry out the role assigned to them, as in many cases in India and other third world countries they do not have any previous experience of working in a group. Generally, the members are poor, illiterate and very unsure of themselves hence they need help to become functional in the group.

Middle Stage

The worker at this stage needs to consolidate the group activities. This can be done by assessing how things are going in the group and making necessary modifications to achieve the group objectives. Even though the worker may be able to initially generate interest in the group activities, the interest can decline if proper planning to maintain it is not done. The monitoring process should commence along with efforts to develop effective leadership in the group.

Monitoring

Monitoring refers to a process of gathering information to keep track of events and activities. The process of gathering information requires working out specific indicators and guidelines and creating systems. It is therefore necessary to be clear about what information is needed and how it would be collected.

Prepare a Profile of Members

- Their educational status
- The general awareness level of group goals
- The self confidence level
- The communication skills
- Interaction with others
- Leadership potential

This profile can serve as the benchmark to see what changes have occurred in individuals as a result of their participation in group activities. The list is not exhaustive the workers can add any other features depending upon the nature of the group.

Develop a system of monitoring the progress of individuals and groups by evolving indicators of change.

For Members

Attendance	*Regular*	*Irregular*	*Absent*
Contribution to group	good	average	poor
Group tasks	good	average	poor
Interaction	very social	average	isolate
Relating to worker	good	average	poor
Relations with members	very social	average	isolate
Others orientation	good	average	poor
Trying to improve self	good	average	poor
Helping others	good	average	poor
Developing norms	good	average	poor
Helping to enforce norms	good	average	poor
Drawing out silent members	good	average	poor
Communication skills	good	average	poor
Others orientation	excessive	moderate	poor
Expertise level needed	excellent	good	average
By the group for task	excellent	good	average
Emotional integration of group	excellent	good	average
Leadership skills	excellent	good	average

For Group

Meetings of Groups	*Very Frequent*	*Frequent*	*Infrequent*
Attendance	well attended	average	poor
Organization	well organized	average	poor
Interaction	warm	average	hostile
Leadership	effective	average	unfocussed
Task accomplishment	good	average	poor
Programme and activities	interesting	average	boring
Programme and activities	Interesting	need based	not focused, catering to segmental needs

The data on most of these indicators can be collected easily as many indicators are self explanatory. However, others orientation and self orientation or personality types, etc., require some skills in measuring them. Others orientation refers to a tendency on the part of an individual to be conscious of other peoples' needs and rights. Self orientation is a tendency to be preoccupied with self interest even at the cost of others. Introversion refers to a person who likes to avoid interaction with others and extroversion refers to a person who loves interaction with others.

The data on all these indicators should be collected on a regular basis and analyzed periodically to assess the change taking place or the progress of the group. The information on the indicators can be collected from different sources such as from members and leaders and from the workers' own observations. The sources can be decided, depending upon the nature of the group and the members. However, it is advisable to use different sources to maintain objectivity and to note how different persons rate the group activities, progress in goal achievement and each other.

Based on these assessments identify potential leaders and training inputs for members as well.

The inputs at this stage will vary, depending upon the objectives the group is focusing on. For example, the self-help groups for providing livelihood or economic benefits to women, are likely to focus on how the savings are progressing, has a bank account been opened, how regularly the meetings are being held, records maintained and so on, while groups formed for children and youth for recreation and education, would focus more on activities and interest level of the members. The middle phase should consolidate the formation stage activities, for example sustaining interest, developing group norms and structure, capacity building inputs to help the members to start functioning more efficiently in the group, development of training inputs and linkages with other organizations to facilitate the group functioning and so on.

Evaluation

Evaluation is an essential part of all processes as it helps the worker and members both, to assess the outcome of their efforts. The critical aspect of evaluation is how objective the evaluation is, what facts have been collected, and the interpretation of facts for drawing a conclusion. The evaluation can be carried out informally or in a formal manner. The professional social workers in India are still working in a more informal environment and have not as yet experienced the pressures of accountability and empirically validated practice. The professional competence can, however, only be proved by showing results, supported by concrete facts. Evaluating the outcomes of interventions, therefore, should be carefully planned and carried out. It will help in improving the professional practice, as we learn what strategies work and the shortcomings. Keeping records is a key area of evaluation. Workers, as we suggested earlier, should learn to develop adequate formats for recording all the happenings in the group.

Format for Recording the Happenings in Each Session

Date............ Time.......... Started............. Time Ended..........Place..........
Names of Members Present
Names of Members Absent
Objective/s of the session ....
Specific goal/s to be achieved ....
Inputs to achieve the goal/s e.g. activities ....
Members' reaction/participation ....
General observation of worker ....
Problems/shortcomings ....

Format for Feedback from Members

Name ....

Kindly provide your feelings about the following aspects of group. This will help in improving the functioning of the group and in meeting your needs in a more focused way.

Do you think the group is doing well?	Yes	Somewhat	No
Do you think other members are helpful to you?	Yes	Somewhat	No
Are the group activities interesting?	Yes	Somewhat	No
Do you think the participation in group is helping you to achieve your needs?	Yes	Somewhat	No
Is the leader helpful?	Yes	Somewhat	No

Any specific problem you would like to share ....
Any specific suggestion to improve the group functioning ....

Although these things can be discussed in an informal feedback session but it may be useful to get a written feedback from all. Despite our best efforts every one may not feel very comfortable being critical in the presence of others. Members may be able to get time to think and provide a more considered opinion if they do it in private. It may also be a more accurate record of how the members feel. The same exercise over a period would show the changes taking place in the members' perception of things in the group.

The evaluation of group work will generally focus on the following points:

- What group goals have been achieved?
- What individual needs have been met?
- What programme and activities have been successful?
- What are the shortcomings?

- What changes will help improve the effectiveness of the intervention?

Make a note covering all the points periodically to keep your records updated.

Source

Sources of evaluation are an important aspect of the evaluation. In working with a group, the worker has access to the group members, the worker's own observations, the records of activities of the group, and other persons who may have interacted with the group or the group members, including the family members. Therefore, a number of sources can be used in finding facts which will help in finding answers to the above questions.

Formal scales or questionnaires for assessment of personality changes, and opinions or attitudes scales can also be used to evaluate the changes in members' knowledge, feeling and attitude levels. It will be useful, however, in such cases to have periodic evaluation.

Each session can also be evaluated with the feedback from members.

Termination Stage

The last stage is the decision to bring the intervention to a close. As we suggested earlier, this may not necessarily mean ending the group in some cases. There may, therefore, be different forms of ending:

- *Withdrawal by the worker and agency:* In this case the worker in the beginning itself may have indicated the overall period of the workers' and agency's association with the group. After the time frame, if the worker is satisfied with the progress of the group, s/he may recommend that the worker and agency will end their direct engagement with the group. However, a more indirect presence or contact with the group may continue. An important aspect of this strategy is to share the evaluation with the group to let them assess their capacity to continue. The worker should plan adequate capacity building inputs during the middle or working phase, to achieve the self-sufficiency in the group. Experiences in all kinds of groups have indicated this to be a very crucial area. Many groups experience a sharp decline after the worker or the organization dilutes its presence. Some organizations have experimented by linking the groups they have formed to create an umbrella network, in order to supervise the functioning of the group in case of self-help groups (see the chapter on self-help groups).

- *Ending the group:* In this case the group comes to an end, as planned. This is generally the case where the group is expected to accomplish some goals within a given time period.
- *Referral:* Referral as a termination strategy is not generally used in case of groups, but in some cases, it may be referred to another organization providing services which the group needs. For example, in a recent case a self help group set up by a student field worker was referred to an organization registering such self-help groups to help them to obtain funds from the rural banks and other government sources. This is a case where the group will continue, although the worker terminates his/her interventions with the group.

Irrespective of the fact what termination strategy is employed, the worker or the leader has to prepare the group for the same. It is better to include it in the planning stage itself and inform the members about the exact nature of the worker and agency support and the duration. The worker should share the final evaluation with the group, to indicate what goals have been achieved and what goals still remain. The worker can help the group to feel good about the success achieved but also help the group to ponder over the shortcomings, both at the individual level and at the group level. In case of groups planning to continue, a task of goal setting can be undertaken to chalk out the future work schedule of the group.

At the termination of a group in particular, an assessment of the individuals' dependence on group should be done carefully. In Indian situation there are examples where members develop very positive emotional ties with each other and find it difficult to end these ties. A successful strategy in such cases has been to keep post-group relations through periodic exchange of messages and occasional meetings if feasible. However, the worker must guard against any emotional overdependence on the part of members, on group, as it can undermine the individuals self reliance and coping capacities.

The groups and members individually can also develop dependence on worker. The worker should carefully monitor this, and take precautions to avoid such a situation. This however generally happens when workers are taking an overactive role to achieve the goals too quickly, and are not allowing the group to work at its own pace. In India, the capacity of members in the groups is generally limited. They need time to learn the art of collective decision-making. They are not familiar with developing procedures or conducting and participating in group discussions. If the worker is not following a process approach and assumes greater responsibility of doing things on behalf of the group rather than helping them to learn, the dependence is inevitable. The workers must learn to keep their anxiety under control, to achieve quick results. Developing leadership among the group members, capacity building of members and developing systems to carry on the functioning of the group, can make the termination smooth.

Post-termination arrangements for monitoring the functioning of the group can also be made, if need be. These are helpful in keeping an updated record of the achievements of the agency and the worker. The groups can also gain by keeping the contact alive in case they may need help in future.

7

Group Work Skills

The term 'skill' refers to the special ability that a person has in carrying out a particular task. All professional workers obtain specific skills relevant to their professional work. There are different ways to identify skills. For example, some scholars identify specific activities such as communicating, attending to feelings, conflict solving, planning, recording and so on, whereas others may concentrate on what we shall refer to as core skills such as communication, listening, analytical thinking, self control and so on. These core skills enable a person to carry out many of the tasks listed above with ease.

A professional approach is characterized by the techniques and skills used to accomplish a task. In identifying the professional skills a reference to tasks is made to highlight the skills by giving details of the actual practice situation. This at times results in confusion between tasks and skills: For example, Corey (2000) identified the following group leadership skills: active listening, restating, clarifying, summarizing, questioning, interpreting, confronting, reflecting feeling, supporting, empathizing, facilitating, initiating, setting goals, evaluating, giving feedback, suggesting, protecting, disclosing oneself, modelling, linking, blocking undesirable behaviour, and Terminating. It is obvious that Corey is identifying the tasks that a group leader has to carry out while leading the group to function smoothly to achieve its objectives. The same tasks can also be defined as the role of a group leader. A closer examination of these tasks reveal that listening, restating, clarifying, summarizing, questioning, and interpreting, in particular, and some other tasks in general, will require an ability on the part of the leader to be able to communicate well – therefore the skill a leader needs to have is communication. But as is obvious there are other abilities, for example, thinking which will help the leader to analyze and understand the persons and their behaviour objectively. Another ability a leader needs to have is how to respond to others to gain their trust, which is so important to influence their behaviour. Therefore, it is obvious that skill is an ability, which helps you to carry out a task or a variety of tasks. The skill of surgery is, for example, used for accomplishing different kinds of tasks. A further expertise to use the skill for carrying a task, for example mending the heart or eye, gives the surgeon a more specific skill of heart surgery or eye surgery, but the basic skill remains surgery. Many other authors like Corey make the mistake of listing all tasks which a group worker has to carry out under the skills. For example, Toseland and Rivas (1995) identified the following group leadership skills: involving group members, attending to others, expressing self, responding to others, focusing group communication, making group processes explicit, or in other words, explaining the group norms, clarifying content, guiding group interactions.

Trecker (1948) has identified the following basic skills of group work: skill in establishing purposeful relationships, skill in analyzing the group situation, skill in participation with the group, skill in dealing with the group feeling, skill in programme development, skill in using agency and community resources, and skill in evaluation.

It is obvious that different authors are identifying different tasks, which they think should be carried out by a worker or leader while working with a group. Further, we can see that skills needed to carry out these tasks in groups are also needed for carrying out similar tasks while working with individuals or communities. I would therefore suggest that we identify core skills needed by social workers and other professionals working with people rather than skills with reference to working with individuals, groups or communities as such. The actual tasks should be identified and discussed separately for clarifying the use of skills in actual practice situation with reference to specific cases and situations.

The core skills that are needed by social workers are the following:

- Communication
- Listening

- Observation
- Analytical thinking
- Empathy
- Self-control
- Leadership

In one of my earlier papers (Siddiqui, 1987) I had identified the core skills as: communication, empathy, observation, listening, and logical reasoning. Communication includes the ability to listen while analytical thinking includes the ability for keen observation of facts as well as remaining objective by exercising control over our passion to construct a reality the way we want to see it. We shall now try and discuss in detail each of these skills. It is generally not realized that the skill to communicate is dependent on the ability of the person to think clearly, the ability of the person to remain in control of her/his feelings and the ability of the person to analyze any situation scientifically. It is therefore obvious that all the skills or in any case many of the skills are interdependent. The discussion on specific skills is however helpful in focusing on different aspects of the ability needed to accomplish different tasks.

Communication

Group workers and all other professionals engaged in any service delivery programme use communication skill to accomplish a number of tasks. Communication generally refers to the ability of a person to convey ideas, facts, fiction and feelings to others. The effectiveness of the communication depends on the degree of its clarity and possibility of distortion in the process commencing from the sender to the receiver. In other words the message conveys what it is expected to convey. For example, the worker wants to convey an idea to the group members. S/he makes a long speech to the group, but the feedback from the members indicate, that the idea has not reached all members or it has conveyed a different meaning, or it has confused the members. This shows that the message has not been conveyed effectively. At a later point of discussion we will analyze why this happened. In order to rectify the situation, the worker or the leader has to restate or re-communicate the message. The task of restating the same statement in groups is needed because some members may not have adequate skills of communication and the way a member or the worker expresses her/his ideas may be beyond the grasp of some members and therefore, evoke a very different response from them. The worker therefore has to intervene by restating or reframing the content of the message to make it more simple for the members. The ability to restate or use the appropriate words is an important part of communication skill. The purpose of an effective communication is to convey the message in such a way that it is understood and accepted by the receiver as being logical and hence to be acted upon or taken note of seriously.

Communication includes both the transference and understanding of meaning. Forms of communication include verbal and nonverbal which include written, audio, audiovisual and body language as well. The communication can be formal and informal. A formal communication originates from a formal source of authority and is usually conveyed in writing or a verbal command from a person placed higher in a formal hierarchy to her/his junior in hierarchy. The components of the communication process are ability to communicate, read, listen and analyze. The process of communication indicates the stages and the medium or channel through which a message passes from the originating source to reach its destination or receiver. The ability to use all mediums of communications such as posters, charts, slides, videos and power points, etc., is an important part of the skill.

According to Robins (1997), communication serves four major functions in a group. They are control, motivation, emotional expression and information.

With reference to Corey's list of activities needed by a group leader, s/he has to listen, restate, clarify, summarize, question, interpret, confront, support, empathize, facilitate, give feedback, suggest, disclose information about self, block undesirable behaviour and so on. In order to carry out these tasks in an effective manner to achieve the desired objective the worker needs the ability to communicate effectively.

Factors Facilitating Communication

The tendency to evaluate and approve is considered a major human barrier in communication (Monappa and Saiyadain, 1994). It is quite common in groups to notice that a member terms the other member or the leader as incompetent. It is obvious that this would have a negative impact on the individual. It is always advisable to avoid using labeling in interpersonal communication in the group. According to communication theory this may happen on account of a number of factors including the members' lack of familiarity with the medium or the language used and the tone or body language. These are just a few observations to indicate how a simple act of conveying an idea may fail if the worker is not a competent communicator.

Using a proper tone while communicating is equally important. It is common to see people making a statement in a loud voice. It is also often the case that the communicator uses a particular tone to communicate her/his displeasure. A professional communicator seldom allows any such occurrence as both indicate that s/he is not in control of her/his feelings.

Objectivity: A major requirement for mastering the art of communication is to be able to observe facts objectively and analyze them logically. Emotional involvement invariably distorts communication. Emotional involvement of the communicator means manipulating the impact of communication. In communication terminology it is called filtering. Filtering refers to a sender manipulating information so that it will be seen more favourably. A leader may, at times pass on information to members which gives them the impression that all is well in the group. It is common to see actors dramatizing a communication in a drama to generate emotions in the audience. It is significant to remember here that the objectivity means that the end results are not manipulated but anticipated.

Clarity about the purpose: The communicator is able to clearly see what message is to be communicated to whom and for what purpose. Knowledge of what is to be communicated is extremely important since, as is common, the message may not be accepted in the first instance and people may want to know more about the message being conveyed. The knowledge in fact gives authenticity to the message. This knowledge makes it easier to communicate since the communication then is spontaneous and not manipulated or superficial. The passion to remain truthful adds further strength to the communication.

Choosing the correct medium: The ability to chose the right medium is equally important. The choice of medium should always be audience focused rather than communicator oriented. The communication is not successful only if it is communicated well. It is successful if it is received and understood well. It is common to see long discussions and no results, yet people can often understand a message without a word being exchanged.

Listening

Listening is a skill, which is available to all of us except those who are impaired in the specific ability but very few of us make full use of it. A professional listener is one who not only receives or gets the content of what is said but also the motivation of the speaker and the reasons for that particular communication of the message. The professional, by using the interactive listening skills, interprets the entire communication immediately by looking at it in a holistic framework. The skill of listening therefore has to be developed by sharpening the analytical skills of content, tone and the body language or facial expressions of the speaker. Listening skills also require the development of sensitivity in the listener to pay attention to the speaker and to respond periodically in an appropriate manner to encourage or convey the fact that s/he is following and understanding the message clearly. The body language has also to reflect that the listener is paying attention to the speaker. At times a proper eye contact and a nod is adequate response to convey that s/he is on the same wavelength as the speaker. In groups it may often happen that many speakers star speaking at once. The group leader is supposed to control the situation, but even in such situation a professional listener is absorbing the relevant content of the speakers and is able to give them cues to encourage them to continue after they get a chance to make their point. This type of response provides assurance to speakers that what they are saying is not only understood but respected. For the listener this also requires learning to focus the mind on the conversation and the actors, and developing an understanding of the vocabulary and cultural symbols used by the members in their normal conversations. The cultural understanding of body language is important; for example, in Hyderabad, a person nods his head from side to side while showing agreement while in north India, in Uttar Pradesh and Bihar particularly, the same gesture is seen as a sign of disagreement. The term 'Bai' is considered a respectable term in Gujarat while it is considered a derogatory term elsewhere for women. Many rural and tribal terms and symbols convey quite different meanings and hence workers having urban backgrounds need to pay special attention to cultural differences in vocabulary and symbols, so as not to be misunderstood.

Observation

Observation refers to the ability of a person to understand things by using simple observation techniques. A keen observer is able to observe small and simple facts which others ignore or consider unimportant. In group work the ability to observe the thinking, feelings and actions of members help the worker to understand them without questioning them. Feelings are difficult to hide and facial expressions and the eyes are gateways to understanding the feelings. A keen observer can always tell if a person is feeling tense, happy or uninterested by looking at him/her. Similarly, the body gestures are good indicators of a person's mood and thinking as well. The worker should be able to observe the changes in the relationships, the morale of the group and so on. Points to remember in developing observation skills are:

- Pay attention to details;
- Concentrate on the finer points rather than generalizing;
- Keep your emotions in check; and
- Be patient.

Analytical Thinking

The intervention by the worker to restate or reframe the communication of members requires an ability on the part of the worker to analyze the communication of each member on the spot and anticipate its impact on the members. This is what is implied by having analytical reasoning skill. The task of summarizing similarly requires the skill on the part of the worker to analyze what the gist of different communications was. The worker in a group is often required to intervene to show that members have deviated from the task. This frequently happens in meetings of the groups called to discuss various issues. It is not uncommon to see that despite a long discussion there is very little progress in the group. The discussion in a group may generate a lot of heat or merrymaking, both of which are likely to deviate the group from its task at hand. The ability of the worker to analyze the situation and to take corrective measures require analytical reasoning. The worker may summarize, restate, interpret, clarify, question or confront the members, in order to accomplish the focus of the group task. All these tasks can be easily carried out with the help of communication and analytical thinking, skill and empathy.

We have still not stated in very specific terms what is analytical thinking. Analytical skill simply refers to maintaining a coherence in interpreting any situation. It also refers to being able to perceive a particular social reality from various perspectives. A simple example can be given that of selecting an appropriate group goal. A member may suggest that the group should help the members in dealing with the poverty situation. The analytical skill of the worker lies in being able to analyze the possibility of keeping it as a group goal. The worker should be able to see the feasibility of achieving the objective in terms of resources available, the expertise and capacities of members, the time frame, the agency objectives in forming the group, and the external and internal environment. Analytical thinking can also be described as raising pertinent questions regarding the problem at hand and being able to find suitable answers as well. Some scholars would simply refer to the skill as the capacity to think straight. This capacity or skill comes with training as also by experiencing different situations and learning from them. The workers have also to control their emotions and feeling to develop analytical skills. In particular anger passion and desire to control situations and persons, can distort your reasoning ability.

Empathy

Empathy refers to the capacity of a person to put oneself in somebody else's situation and understand the feelings and emotions involved. It is often referred to as an intuitive feeling of others emotions and feelings. A worker should be skillful in anticipating how individuals express themselves, deal with tension and conflict, defend themselves in face of being threatened, etc. In dealing with children in difficult circumstances and women in particular this skill is most often tested. The problems and tensions that a child on the street goes through in places like Mumbai, Delhi, Chennai, Colombo, Karachi or Dhaka cannot be easily understood by a person who has never faced such a situation personally. Similarly, the fear and trauma of sexual harassment and abuse faced by females in the lower socio economic strata is difficult to understand or visualize by a male worker. The effect it is likely to have on the interaction of females in a group, for example, in a panchayat (village level local body organization in India) meeting or Gram Sabha (village general body) meeting can only be understood through empathy. We also need a realistic understanding of the torture and exploitation that Dalits have undergone in India. Empathy is the real test of our ability to realize the sufferings that others have experienced or the dilemmas and tensions and uncertainty that others have faced which we have been fortunate to escape.

The skill of empathy can be developed first by becoming aware of the differences that are characteristic of the lives of people of different strata in society. The next step is accepting and respecting these differences. A simple example is the cultural differences between tribal, rural and urban population within the same region, the gender differences, caste, religious and linguistic differences and so on. The class differences are also very important. An empathetic understanding begins with an awareness that not all people think similarly, or have similar feelings or ways of thinking or looking at things. Similarly, the fact that not all people possess the capabilities one may consider either normal or common abilities to accomplish different task. A conscious realization of these facts will help in understanding the differences in reactions of people, which may not be in conformity with common standards. In Indian context, where cultural differences are so much in evidence, a worker should be careful in making a remark like "you can't even do such a simple thing".

Self-Control

Another common human weakness in the Indian subcontinent is allowing emotions to take over the rational mind. People are quite prone to feel annoyed, happy, violence-prone or depressed in a variety of situations. The first indicator of the condition where a person has lost self direction or control is the tension which is reflected in one's thinking, feeling and action. Suppose, a worker is trying to organize a meeting of the group but only a few members have turned up after almost half an hour has gone past the schedule time. The worker starts shouting at the members present and complaining about the lack of responsible behaviour on their part. This is a sign of loss of self-control. For example, group of children playing a game start a fight among themselves. The worker may show anger at the happening or may even punish one or two children. These instances are a clear indication of the worker losing self-control and get this carried away. The need to do something about the situation is obvious, but in group work, the worker is primarily there to help the members to do things on their own and try and find ways of finding solutions to the problem. The worker can suggest or invite suggestions from the group to deal with situations but if s/he shows anxiety about events and behaviour of group members it is indicative of lack of self-control. A professional is expected to have full control over emotions and feelings, and to be able to act objectively and effectively.

How do we develop the skill of self-control?

The development of a professional self is an important aspect of a professional training programme. The first step is to differentiate personal from professional. All human beings develop specific values about different aspects of life situations. It is a natural process of our growing up. Culture plays an important part in developing these value preferences. This makes us accustomed to treating certain behaviours as desirable and others, in varying degrees, as either tolerable or to be denounced. As an individual we have the freedom to exercise our opinions, but as a professional we are guided by professional values where a deliberate attempt must be made to keep these non-judgmental to the maximum extent possible. However, exercising control on our behaviour requires that we become aware of our weaknesses. It is common to get swayed by our need to talk, to control things, to be hurt by criticism or opposition to our ideas, and so on. A review of our own behaviour after some sessions with groups is helpful in making us aware of the areas, which may need change and modification. Awareness and later a determined effort to achieve professional competence through continuous review and practice is a good way to bring about improvements.

Leadership

Leadership, as a professional role, is the process of guiding the development of the group and its members (Toseland and Rivas, 1995). The process of guiding involves a number of activities such as:

- Clarifying the objectives of the group to members;
- Involving the members in the group activities;
- Focusing the communication in the group;
- Guiding group interaction; and
- Resolving conflicts;

- Analyzing different aspects of issues being handled by the group, and so on.

However, as we mentioned earlier, we are looking at the leadership skill as such rather than the skill of carrying out all the activities separately. A person possessing leadership skill will be able to carry out all these activities with professional ease and competence. The issue often asked is whether leaders are born or any one can be a leader if s/he made an effort to become one. It is possible that some persons are born with characteristics or traits that are helpful in becoming a leader, but generally, other traits are acquired through education, training and socialization. The skill of leadership can be developed and workers working with a group have a firm belief in the ability of members to carry out leadership roles. There are different types of leadership roles needed for the development of the group, a point which is missed by many leaders themselves. For example, a person may be good in providing guidance to the group about how to interact with each other, how to respond to the needs and feelings of others and needs in the group, but s/he may not have any technical expertise to resolve economic issues being faced by the members. The concepts of co-leadership or rotating leadership or a flat structure in the group, all refer to using the resources of all and involving and recognizing the contribution of everyone, is the preferred style of leadership in social work groups. Toseland and Rivas (1995) conceptualize leadership skill in three parts. They are: facilitating group processes, data collection and assessment and action. Harvey J. Bertcher (1994), gives a long list of activities beginning from attending, seeking and giving information, rewarding, modeling, mediating, responding to feelings, focusing, summarizing, etc., rather than any broad aspects of leadership. Corey and Corey (2006) focus on attitudes and actions needed by the leader and generally identify different roles for the leader at different stages of group development.

In the beginning stage, they suggest building trust by listening attentively and understanding non-verbal behaviour, developing empathy, genuineness and making self disclosure, respecting others and creating a caring confrontation with members, clarifying goals, developing group norms and cohesion, etc. At the transition stage, the group leader's roles include handling defensiveness and resistance of members by dealing with their fears, maintaining a sense of control by handling conflicts and confrontations, handling difficult members, silence and non participation, and monopolistic behaviour, etc. (for details see Corey and Corey, 2006). The authors then suggest that the leader has to make certain choices at the working stage i.e., between disclosure and anonymity, spontaneity versus control, acceptance versus rejection and so on. The roles at the final stage begins with consolidation of learning, dealing with feelings of separation, reviewing group experiences, dealing with setbacks, and so on. These descriptions help us to focus on a number of activities which a leader is expected to perform in the group.

The development of leadership skills, therefore, should commence with reviewing the various roles that a leader is expected to play. The next step is to review your personal resources to see how comfortable you are in carrying out the roles. It is equally important to see the level of your commitment to the group objectives and your ability to accept all members. At first review you may find some inadequacies but that is normal. Very few persons are perfect. A good self-review is very empowering and helps in improving and learning. Maintaining a positive flexible attitude is important for carrying out any leadership role effectively.

8

Techniques of Working with Groups

Techniques are interventions aimed at facilitating movement within a group (Corey and Corey, 2006). They go on to suggest that almost anything that a worker or leader does in a group can be considered as a technique, including the use of silence. However, there are various techniques that are used more often by workers to facilitate their work with groups. It is however important to remember that the techniques are used in the context of the insights gained from the principles and process details. Some of the more frequent techniques used by the workers in working with the groups are:

- Group Counselling
- Group Discussion
- Decision-making
- Role Play
- Programme Media: Play and Games, Story Telling, Singing, Theatre, Art & Craft, Poster Making, Collage, etc.
- Individual Sessions

Group Counselling

Group counselling refers to activities that are used to enrich members' capacities through skill building or helping them to achieve changes in their behavioural patterns to achieve a better mental heath status. The frameworks generally used to do counselling differ from worker to worker. Some of the well-known examples are where all three, i.e., cognitive, affective and behavioural domains are dealt with by a worker. The distinguishing feature of the group counselling is that the group environment is used to accomplish both development of life skills and accomplish and strengthen changes among members.

Group counselling therefore is a group process to accomplish changes in the way people think, feel and act. The group participates in the developmental, behavioural, and attitudinal concerns of the individual members of the counselling group.

Using Activity in Group Counselling

One of the first to recommend the use of activity as a means of creating a therapeutic climate was Moreno (1946). Moreno's activity-oriented approach led to the development of socio-drama and psychodrama. Slavson (1954), however, pioneered and expanded the application of media such as arts and crafts, table games, and outdoor activities such as field trips and excursions in the treatment of adolescents and children. Slavson (1945) pointed out how different set of activities are valuable for groups of different ages?

What little children gain through play and acting out, young children in their latency period and early adolescence achieve through manual activity, creative expression, and free play and interaction with one another. Older adolescents and adult, however, are more prone to use verbal expression and insight to gain the same results. This model of group counselling also termed as activity-interview-group counselling, an activity, is used to involve the group and to lower the inhibitions and defenses of the group members. The activity itself generally provides an opportunity for physical catharsis or release of tension. It serves the same purpose as systematic desensitization practiced by behaviourally oriented workers and therapists. In addition to providing a means for tension reduction through physical catharsis, the activity provides an opportunity for interpersonal interactions, which are the concern of the worker and members in the group discussions following the game or activity. Activities may be many and varied. The group should choose the activities according to the needs of the members. Care should be taken to vary the games or activities in order to provide suitable experiences to all members of the group. Athletic children should have the opportunity to demonstrate their talents in team sports like cricket, football, kho-kho, kabaddi and volleyball. Similarly, less athletic children should have an opportunity to experience success in carrom, chess, table tennis, etc. Still other activities such as singing, and arts and crafts should be used for those who may have talents apart from the physical. Since the activity itself, in activity based group counselling represents only part of the intervention program, those activities that involve simultaneously several if not all the group members should be most used. The discussion or interview group counselling session following the game or activity, constitutes the second part of the treatment. During this period the worker helps the group members focus on the nature of the interactions and the behaviour that occurred during the activity phase. The behaviour that occurred during the activity is related to the lifestyle of a given group member. The worker builds a strong facilitative base with high levels of empathy, respect, and warmth; only after having established a feeling of mutual trust and care does the worker move the group members into the planning and action phase.

The interview or discussion phase need not be held in a formal setting such as a conference room, although such a room should be available when movement from an activity setting is required. The conference room can also be set up as a dual-purpose room that contains equipment and materials for group activities as well as chairs for the interview phase.

Group Counselling for Adults

The adults have achieved a stage in their development where the most natural and efficient communication medium is language or verbalizing. Thus, with this age group, group counselling is the preferred mode of intervention. The counselling model focusing on counselee verbalization is the *Cognitive-Behaviour Model* of Meichenbaum (1977). He terms his model as an integrative approach as it deals with both cognitive and affective domains and then with coping response mediated through these domains (Meichenbaum, 1977).

The change process consists of three phases, according to Meichenbaum. These phases, he cautions, are not compartments, but are interwoven. Phase 1 is self-observation. In this first step, the counselee becomes an observer of his or her own behaviour. The purpose is self-exploration. Typically, the counselee is in a state of confusion when he or she comes for counselling; his or her thoughts and behaviours are frequently maladaptive and lead to a sense of helplessness and despair. In order to change it the counselee must learn to produce thoughts and behaviours by using a different cognitive framework. The group environment is used to help the counselee to discover the alternative framework to structure the thoughts and feelings in order to provide a new and more satisfying experience to the person.

The counselee usually comes to counselling with some conceptualization of his or her problems. This conceptualization must undergo change if the counselee is to change. This change is mediated by the interaction between counselee and worker and other counselees. The re-conceptualization that takes place is one in which the counselee redefines the problem and as a result gains a sense of control and hope, which are both necessary if change is to occur. Meichenbaum emphasizes the importance of self-direction the counselee has to use to accomplish change. What he or she is saying to himself or herself about the maladaptive behaviour is very important. The counselee, the worker and the group should work to evolve a common conceptualization, where the counselee is an active participant. The client thus comes to view his problem from a different perspective, helping him to arrive at a new explanation for the etiology and maintenance of his maladaptive behaviour (Meichenbaum, 1977: 223).

Phase 2 concerns the counselee's initiating the cognitions and behaviours that deal effectively with the maladaptive behaviour. It is like asking oneself "what do I achieve by being negative in my approach?" As the client's self-observations become more directed towards controlling aspects of his maladaptive behaviour, the client learns to initiate new cognitions and behaviours. The self-exploration signals the opportunity for producing the adaptive thoughts and behaviours.

Phase 3 of the model deals with the review of the outcomes of these *"experiments"*. Meichenbaum refers to this third phase as *"cognitions concerning change"*. He emphasizes that in this phase, it is not enough to produce adaptive acts through skill training; rather it is the phase of self-conviction, that is, how the counselee addresses him/her self, about these acts or behaviours. The reactions from others in the group will determine whether the behaviour will persist and generalize. Meichenbaum contends that intervention is not successful until both the counselee's behaviour and internal dialogue change.

Developmental Group Counselling

The developmental group counselling believes in giving better life-skills to people to handle their social functioning problems, either current or future. As such it may or may not deal with individual problems of members but enable them to become capable of dealing with all their problems through a process of self-exploration, handling their communications better and exercising a better control over their feelings particularly under stress. The model also includes teaching new attitudes and behaviour based on a consistent model for given life-skill areas. The developmental model operates on the assumption that the counselee can accept the rationale offered for a given life-skill area. For example, if the life-skill deficit area is interpersonal communication/human relations, the model that the group leader chooses to teach the group must be logical and meaningful to the counselees before they will learn it. If it is too esoteric or appears unrelated to the counselees' deficit, the members will not make the necessary effort to learn the model. Once the model is learned, it will be used in all situations.

Information Model of Group Counselling

In this model of group counselling the worker simply provides information to the group members about where the deficit is anticipated. The group members have the advantage of discussing the information and its implication in their personal life with other group members who are guided by the worker to respond in an appropriate manner. The worker also participates along with any experts called for the purpose of providing information in the group counselling. The general areas where this model has been found to be of help by group workers are health related issues, legal issues relating to marriage, divorce and inheritance, economic issues, career counselling, etc.

Group Discussion

Group discussion is a vital means of communicating and sharing of ideas in a group. The group is a forum for making decisions, solving problems faced by its members both individually and collectively, promoting growth, and accomplishing a variety of objectives. The group discussion as a technique, helps in developing appropriate attitudes and skills of members since they learn to look at a problem from several perspectives, appreciate diversity in view points and grant equal opportunities for all to express and be heard. The participation in group discussion helps members to develop self respect and a positive self concept, as they realize that they have the ability to solve problems or express themselves in a manner which others appreciate. An experience of participating in group discussion is a lesson in democratic functioning. The ability to accept criticism is a very enabling experience and is much easier to learn through a good group discussion. The workers use group discussion for a variety of purposes to keep the group moving towards its objectives.

Planning

Trecker (1948) realized the importance of group discussion in working with groups and therefore gave a great deal of thought to carrying out discussions in the group. One of the suggestions he made was that it is important to analyze the background of the members in order to assess their competence for participation in group discussion. Factors such as their educational status, experience of participation in groups, their family and social background, communication skill and so on, are important indicators of a person's ability to participate in group discussions. The worker therefore must plan the group discussion based on the capacity of the members. Trecker suggested a simple formula of choosing simple issues in the beginning and move on to more complex issues for discussion as the group progresses towards maturity. In fact, a calm and relaxed environment during the discussion can be taken as an indicator of group development as well.

Setting

Setting for group discussion is an important aspect of planning. The preferred setting is a circular seating arrangement where members can clearly see each other. The circle should be close enough to enable each member to hear and observe each other's body gestures and facial expressions. The worker or leader should try to maintain an equidistant position to the maximum extent possible. Audio-visual arrangements are helpful but in Indian situations more indigenous ways of visual materials should be used keeping in view the resource level available at rural and deprived urban neighbourhood sites.

Agenda

Agenda is an important part of planning the discussion. The subjects for discussion should be listed according to the priority of the issues. Both strategies of listing important topics first or last have been followed by workers depending on their understanding of the members' behaviour. In some discussions there is a tendency on the part of the members to show more enthusiasm in the beginning. As the time progresses and energy levels get depleted they tend to slow down. Other groups take a slow start and gradually warm up to participate more actively. The worker should make sure that the group has enough time for discussing the agenda, which means that agenda should be neither too long nor too short, giving members the feeling that the meeting ended rather quickly. Controversial issues that generate debate should be anticipated and provided should be enough time for meaningful discussion rather than hurrying the debate which may leave some people feeling dissatisfied with the outcome and for not getting a chance to express their views. Prior intimation about the topics for discussion is considered essential for the success of discussion since it provides enough time to members to think. However, in a children's group, discussions are more spontaneous and may not follow a very formal structure. The worker, however, should always be prepared and should organize the discussions according to a carefully planned agenda.

Supervision

Group discussions have little chance of success without adequate supervisory inputs. All discussions in the group should be presided over by a group member, leader or the worker depending on the nature of the group and the discussion. Even in very informal discussions it is better to have a person coordinating the discussions. The supervisor helps the group to participate in an orderly manner. S/he clarifies the purpose of discussion, helps the member in understanding the issues being discussed, summarizes the discussion, helps members to; discuss the issues and not the person, keeping their comments brief without repeating or overstating a point already made, not allowing their emotions to overshadow their objectivity, respecting diversity, seeking permission before speaking up and always addressing the chair rather than individual members. S/he prevents overdomination by one or few members and encourages the somewhat passive members to participate. The supervisor also either makes arrangements for recording the main points of the discussions or keep notes to later prepare a proper record of the discussion. In informal discussions the detailed minutes may not be needed but it always helps the worker in assessing or evaluating the group functioning if some record of all discussions held in the group are kept. The supervisor and worker both have a crucial role to play in the group. *Problems* generally encountered by the worker in the group are:

- *Silence:* One of the common problems in discussion are long periods of silence. This indicates either lack of interest on the part of members, the inability of the members to understand the issue at discussion, lack of adequate communication skills or exposure to participation in groups, fear of the worker, leader or others in the group, which is also known as a hostile environment, or any other factor. Some suggestions to handle the problem have already been discussed, such as helping the members to understand the issue, keeping the agenda simple and relevant to the needs of the members and the group and so on. The handling of a hostile environment is done by developing appropriate norms and by taking care at the time of formation of the group to keep the diversity among members to a manageable proportion. Capacity building and networking among members are also useful strategies to empower members to deal with opposition.
- *Lack of movement:* Discussions getting out of hand or stagnated is a common occurrence as members deviate from the main issues under discussion. The need to talk on the part of members or chair, to make an impression on other members or worker, insecurity, lack of focus, etc., can result in the discussion-making no progress. This can be avoided by restricting the members and reminding them to be brief and focused. A good summarization of the discussion also helps in facilitating the movement in the discussion. Lack of expertise in the group to tackle the problem or issue can also lead to stagnation in the discussion.
- *Over domination:* The very term indicates the nature of the problem and effective supervision can easily avoid the problem. However, the worker needs to be polite and diplomatic to contain such members and to avoid hurting their genuine enthusiasm at

times. It may also be kept in mind that some members are always more active participants than others and it is natural among human groups to have this diversity. The supervisor or worker can also develop a tendency to dominate the discussion. This is very harmful for group discussion as it can kill the very spirit of group discussion. The only way it can be prevented is self analysis by the supervisor and worker and vigilance on the part of members to bring this out in the open for discussion by the group. Dissent based on facts is a potent strategy in such cases, which helps to contend the overdomination by the chair.

- *Personality-centred:* Group discussion can become personality-centred in situations where subgroups become more strong and tend to undermine group cohesion. These situations generally arise when members are not sure about the group goals and how the achievement of goals would be shared among the members (for a detailed discussion on sub group formation see the chapter on processes). The supervisor can help the members to take note of the mistake they are making and how it can affect the group functioning. S/he should encourage other members to intervene and express their disagreement with such behaviour.

Group Decision-Making

Group decision-making is the process of arriving at a decision where more than two individuals are involved. The process of decision-making is a key component to understand the functioning of a group. Decision-making patterns can be used to develop an understanding of effective group functioning. In general, group decision-making patterns based on what is the manner of decision-making can be identified. These patterns are described in the chapter on group processes.

Group performance is largely dependent upon the decision-making processes that a particular group uses. If the group takes decisions which are not based on facts the chances of the success of the group are limited. Similarly, if the decisions are taken keeping the interest of only a section of the group members, other members are not likely to benefit from these decisions giving rise to conflicts in groups. In every group, decisions have to be made on a number of issues involving groups functioning. These decisions range from what goals the group should have, who should be the leader of the group or when and where the group should meet, etc. The decisions involves resources (i.e., in the form of time and energy) of the members. The decisions involve the future of the group in terms of what would happen in the group and who would control it.

As the examples illustrate, the decisions and the processes involved in making them are not limited to any one individual. The decision-making process is performed at the group level. Since the resources involved in the group decision-making process as well as the impact of these decisions affect group performance, it is crucial to make the group decision-making process as participatory, efficient and effective as possible. Many a time the groups may not even be aware of what kind of model of decision-making they are using generally in making the decisions.

The model being followed in the group will indicate what is the current pattern of taking decisions and what role the members are playing in it. Is the model helpful in the group development or would it create or is already creating problems. Analysis of this kind can help the group to address the task of evaluating the manner of decision-making, with a view to make it more efficient and to make it conform to the needs of the group.

Another aspect of the group decision-making is to assess it in terms of the capacity levels of different members and the participation level. It is obvious that the level of participation will have a positive correlation with the capacity of the members to understand the issues and be able to communicate their opinions. The decision-making process also reveal the nature of power members enjoy and its use or misuse. In India the decision-making in groups represents a very wide variety. The groups in formal settings such as formal organizations is very different than what is found in groups formed by social workers or other professionals working with deprived populations. While the groups in formal settings are likely to be influenced by formal leaders or managers and may generally follow the rational or process model, the ones formed by workers of different kind usually follow the directions and guidance provided by the worker and follow the rational or political model.

A worker must always be alert to discover:

- That the group environment is conducive to a democratic decision-making process.

- That the group effort at problem solving or decision-making is proving to be time consuming and costly without yielding a result which works.
- Not every one knows how to help a group in taking a decision quickly and rationally.
- The expertise in the group may not exist to take certain decisions.

Role Play

Role playing is a creative way of helping the members to look at their own behaviour and how others view it. In role play a real life situation is simulated. The technique has been found to be helpful in dealing with stress and learning new coping strategies. Role plays require careful planning like the group discussion. The purpose of the role play should be carefully decided and accordingly the situation to be simulated should be selected. A good example is a child's interaction with a friend, teacher or parent. A young man's experience with opposite sex, a discussion between husband and wife, people losing self control in facing some situations, or any other situation highlighting a particular behaviour creating problems can be selected. A complete script with detailed dialogues should be developed. A careful selection of actors to carry out the role play and to provide them feedback after seeing their performance can help improve the quality. Other members can also participate as observers. The role play should be followed by discussion based on observer's report and how the members react to the situation presented through role play. A safe and friendly environment is crucial for the success of the role play.

Yet another method of using role play in a group is to first provide an opportunity to all the members to narrate any situation, particularly a relationship which they find it difficult to handle. Record the discussion among the group members. Create role plays based on the discussion. Each member should first be asked to act as self in the role play. The role should then be reversed for the member to experience how the other party feels or views his/her behaviour. An open discussion and comments session should follow. Later each member should be asked to identify the changes which s/he thinks will help to deal with the situation, which could again be shared in the group. The group can offer suggestions and help all members to report progress in the subsequent sessions.

Sensitivity training is a useful use of role play as well. All of us are sensitive to certain stimuli which evoke certain reactions from us. A simple example is that not all of us are able to accept criticism gracefully. In a group, a situation can be created where a member is subjected to a situation where s/he has to face criticism from others. The member is forewarned to control her/his reactions. Different levels of anxiety would be exhibited by the person undergoing the exercise. These can be categorized as level I to level III. Level I is total lack of control, level II is partial control and level III is full control over one's behaviour resulting in a mature response to the criticism. These exercises should be repeated in subsequent sessions till the person achieves some progress. The level of criticism can also be increased or decreased depending on the progress or capacity of the person.

Programme Media

Programme media refers to all those activities such as games, singing, craft activities, story telling, street plays, other theatre activities, etc., which workers organize in groups to generate interaction among members to accomplish a number of objectives in the group. These activities help the individuals to become a group. The group then makes the individuals. The influence of the group on members lies in three areas: participation in activities, interaction with other members and their interaction with the worker.

Games in particular provide an opportunity for children to express their feelings and exhibit behaviour which is frank and a true expression of what is lying dormant inside. A number of games, both indoor and outdoor can be organized. In India outdoor games such as cricket, football, kabbadi and kho kho are very popular and do not require costly resources. Other outdoor games are dividing the group in two teams and making them compete in picking up an object from a central place.

There are a number of games where tasks can be assigned to each team such as collecting small balls of different colours from a container, putting thread into a set of needles, filling up water in a bucket by using small spoons, making a square from jumbled pieces without talking to each other and so on. Four to five pieces of squares are cut into pieces (see Figure 1). The pieces are mixed and distributed in four or five envelops. Each member is given an envelop. Each member of the group has to complete his square. The group whose members complete their task first wins. The rules are the members cannot talk to each other, but they are permitted to pass on the piece if they do not need it, to the member on their left. These games are specifically meant to give the members an experience of accomplishing tasks in a group by focusing on group objectives. It also provides an experience of sharing in the group achievement.

Figure 1

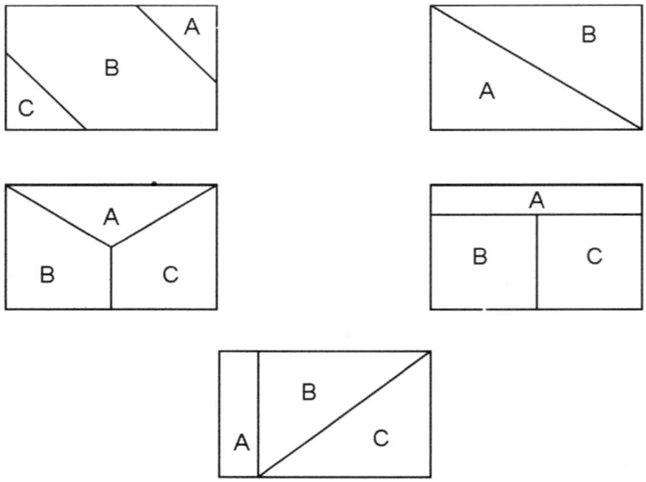

Indoor games by using pencil and paper or cards can be devised by workers to generate general knowledge and fun. A popular game is to distribute cards to members and ask them to describe a member by using a label. Each member then is given a chance to identify the member who is given the label. The caution is to explain to group not to give negative labels but ones that convey some specific behaviour pattern of the member that can serve as a feedback [see Dwivedi (2005) for more details on games and other activities with children and adolescents].

Singing and storytelling are other activities which can be carried out in groups. Storytelling and writing stories can be carried out by encouraging children and adolescents to create their own stories by narrating their own interesting episodes in life. They can also be given half the story and asked to complete the rest of the story.

Play and theatre activities are very popular activities with groups of children and adolescents. The worker can select plays specifically written for children or create plays, generally small skits, through a participatory exercise in the group. Enacting real-life situations from school, office or even from family, are very interesting ways of helping them to reflect on these situations and also how to deal with them. Writing the dialogues, designing the stage, distributing roles, acting on stage all these go a long way in providing a number of very meaningful experiences to children and adolescents.

Special care should be taken to select activities for physically and mentally challenged children, and for children having experienced trauma in the recent past.

Art and craft are also used in groups for engaging members and helping them to express themselves. Poster making around any popular theme is a popular activity. A collage can be made from pictures or other material to focus attention on any particular problem.

Individual Sessions

Individual sessions are also used by workers while working with groups for a variety of objectives, in particular to handle the needs of individual members to carry on their fruitful participation in group. Treatment groups in particular need individual sessions but at times other groups such as even a self-help group may need some interview sessions with individuals.

Planning

Like all other activities an interview requires careful planning. The worker has to plan in advance the setting for holding the session, and also its content and the follow up action in order to achieve the expected outcome. The worker has to assess the capacity of the individual very carefully to plan the content. The time management is a crucial part of the planning. The worker should have enough time to deal with the session as most sessions may not end as per the scheduled time. Yet it is necessary to have a time schedule for all sessions, which should be developed in a participatory manner keeping the individual's convenience in mind.

Objectives

The sessions with individuals are held for any or all of the following objectives:

- Assessment of individual for inclusion in the group.
- Assessment of individual's needs/ problems.
- Providing support to individuals to make best use of group experiences.
- Getting feedback.

The selection of group members is important in all kinds of groups but more in treatment groups. A certain amount of planning is necessary, to avoid extreme differences which may create a problem in working together later. Individual sessions, are therefore needed to make an assessment of the individual characteristics. Many group workers organize a bigger group where all intending members are placed. The individual sessions are organized after observing the individuals in the group for some time. Use of various kinds of tools for assessment of the individual is also very common. We have already referred to some tools in the discussion on social science findings on groups. More recent tools developed to measure different behavioural aspects can be used but it may be advisable to test the appropriateness of the tool before its use. It is also helpful to use other experts to get necessary inputs if need be, both for assessment and for the follow up action to be taken.

Group workers have to hold individual sessions in working with groups to assess individual needs and problems as well. The group is generally used as a forum to encourage members to express their needs and problems but some times some members need special help in expressing their needs. However, the use of the individual sessions should be done after careful assessment and with the knowledge of the group. In fact, it may be necessary to develop it as a group norm that members can make use of individual attention from the leader or the worker if needed. The worker will have to accordingly schedule the time in the work schedule. Since the problems of the individual will vary according to the kind of client group and the purpose of the group, with which the worker is working. The worker will accordingly make a decision regarding what approach to adopt to deal with the problem. Selecting a relevant approach and being clear about the factors causing problem will be helpful in dealing with the problems. There is enough evidence to suggest that the thinking pattern and feelings of people influence their actions (Meichenbaum, 1977; Toseland and Rivas, 2001). A number of techniques are now available to alter cognitive and affective development (see chapter on assumption and theories).

Some members need special support for sorting out their difficulties in participating in the group as such. Individual sessions are needed for preparing members to take part in role plays, sensitivity training and helping to overcome other anxieties. Instances of members remaining quiet most of the time or exhibiting a very passive approach in all group activities reflect the existence of anxieties and doubts. These members may not request the worker or leader for help. In such cases the worker will have to be careful in monitoring these individuals. At times over active and members trying to dominate the group activities may also need individual sessions, if the group is not able to suitably modify their behaviour. The worker should remember that the group can be effectively used in many cases to prevent the use of individual sessions.

Evaluation of group activities is a necessary part of work with the group. One of the sources of information for evaluating the group activities, the worker's/leader's inputs, general environment in the group, and the members' own reaction to participation in group are the members of the group. The feedback from members as such, is a well accepted method of collecting information. The information is collected in group orally as also in written form. Individual sessions may be held for refining the quality of this information. At times confidentiality can bring out information which otherwise may not be shared. Many individual find it difficult to share their personal feelings openly. Individual sessions are helpful in helping people to share their objective assessment.

Process

The individual sessions should be carefully planned as suggested earlier. The group worker should work out the details of the process depending upon the objective of the individual session. The worker already has a relationship with the member, and it helps in getting the first session going smoothly. Even then the worker must clarify the objective of the session to the individual, answer any queries, and help the individual to relax. The worker can collect information or facts in a planned manner with the help of a guideline. The information can also be given at a pace so that the person can easily follow and the chances of distortions are minimized. The person should be allowed enough time to express his/her problem and an analysis of the problem should be made and shared with the person. The outcome of the session, should be assessed to see if any subsequent sessions are needed. As suggested earlier, the individual should be helped to focus on how s/he can use the group to meet his/her needs and seek a solution to the problem by using the group.

A record of the session should also be kept.

9

Group Work with Children, Adolescents and Elderly

Group work as a method to provide developmental inputs to children and adolescents can be used to achieve a number of objectives. The actual nature of interventions will differ since at least three broad categories of children and adolescents can be identified, who will require different kinds of inputs through group work. These categories are, normal children and adolescents, children in need of care and protection but not living in institutions, and children and adolescents in residential care institutions. In all the categories, the focus is generally on children between the preadolescent ages, varying from 9 to 14 years of age, and adolescents in the age group of 15 to 25.

The Context of Group Work Practice with Children and Adolescents in India

Children and adolescents constitute a significant part of all societies. In many developing societies they constitute around 40-50 per cent of the population. The social and economic progress of a country, to a great extent, depends upon the development inputs provided to this segment of the society. Group work as a method can be used to work with this significant population to provide a number of services that will ensure a solid foundation of human and social capital in the country.

Social Environment

The social environment of children and adolescents like the family, school, peer groups, and neighbourhood environment, play a vital part in their overall development. The impact of these social units (some authors refer to these as social systems) on children and adolescents, can be both positive and negative. The importance of childhood experiences and socialization during adolescence has been highlighted in a number of studies. It is generally acknowledged that they can be vital in shaping the social behaviour in later life. Poor and broken families and deprived neighbourhoods are known for their inability to ensure adequate development inputs for children and youth. The deprived neighbourhoods expose children and youths to a number of stressful situations, which could be very harmful for them. Extreme poverty, broken families leading to poor parenting, family violence, alcoholism and tobacco use at an early age leading to health problems, lack of education, and physical and sexual abuse, are fairly common problems in such neighbourhoods. The lack of proper guidance and caring are identified as causes of their coming in conflict with law. Such children constitute a sizeable number in developing countries including India. Even in affluent families children and youth may need capacity building in many life skill areas such as accepting diversity, exercising self control and handling conflicts. Group work can be used, for providing timely help to such children in India and other developing countries.

Residential homes are another setting where group work can prove helpful in providing development inputs for children and youths. The children and adolescents coming in conflict with law or those needing shelter are placed here for providing them development inputs to mainstream them into the society. However, the current situation in some of these institutions are an impersonal environment, over crowding and violence. At times there is overstrictness on the part of the staff, which itself generates a lot of stress for children and adolescents. In developing countries there is always shortage of trained staff to handle the individual needs and problems of these children and adolescents. The possibility of individual counselling interventions is rather remote. Group interventions are more feasible, and particularly groups composed of persons facing similar problems are known to exert a vital influence on the behaviour of group members. Group work therefore, offers a much better option for helping the inmates of a residential institution in developing countries.

Educational Setting

Schools and colleges provide significant inputs in developing human capital in the society. As Reimer (1971) noted, the level at which a child drops out from the school will determine whether s/he will work with his/her hands or mind, and what social roles and status s/he will be accorded. Many a time neither the parents nor the teachers are aware of the fact that the child is facing stress in school. Even if they do, they are not proficient in dealing with the problem. The sources of stress may vary from scholastic difficulties to the problem of maintaining relationships. The organizational dynamics of schools also makes an impact on the social and academic adjustment of children and adolescents (Hannan and Freeman, 1984). School policies such as rules for conduct and manner of rule enforcement, number of teachers, their training and educational status, etc., all of these can be potential sources of stress. Pressure from parents and teachers for achieving high standards of academic performance and social behaviour, are the most common sources of stress. Girls in particular, cutting across all socio economic strata, caste and religious categories, face a higher level of stress from some of these sources. The stress, faced by children if left unattended, may lead to mental health problems and drop outs. Guidance and support is an effective way of dealing with stress, and group is an ideal medium to provide both. Ensuring educational inputs to children outside the formal school setting also poses a serious challenge in all developing societies. The group work offers a useful opportunity in addressing many of these issues.

Objectives

The success of the group work depends to a great extent on the clarity of the objectives. The first question a child is likely to ask is, what activities is the group going to have? If the activities are not interesting, the child is not likely to join the group. In case s/he comes in, s/he is not likely to stay in the group for long. Studies on working with groups indicate that the individuals joining the groups show a great deal of variety in their objectives. The group objective should be broad enough to cover these individual differences of needs. A need assessment of potential members, as suggested in the chapter on process, would be helpful in framing the objectives. Some of the common needs of children in India and other developing countries are: recreation, education, companionship, security, recognition, caring, etc. In addition, support in case of emotional trauma from family violence or lack of family, is also a major need area. The objective of group work with children, will however, depend on the kind of children the worker is working with. The purpose of the group is generally also influenced by the sponsoring organization. Some group work objectives of working with children are suggested below. The list is by no means exhaustive, it is only suggestive. A number of other objectives can also be identified to work with groups of children. What is important to remember is to have definite objectives, identify them carefully, share them with the group, and keep them flexible.

Group Work with Normal Children

- To provide recreational services to children
- To provide an experience of functioning in groups
- To provide informal education
- To prepare children for social responsibility
- To develop life skills
- To provide help in dealing with problems of social functioning

Group Work with Street and Working Children

- To provide recreational activities
- To meet emotional needs of children
- To develop life skills to strengthen capacities to avoid exploitation and abuse
- To provide livelihood and shelter
- To provide informal education

Group Work with Children in Residential Institutions

- To provide recreational activities
- To develop life skills to strengthen their capacities to manage life in an institution
- To provide help in dealing with personal problems
- To provide informal education
- Emotional support

The objectives listed above suggest that group work with children will involve both task-oriented and treatment-oriented group work. We will first discuss the task oriented activities with children in general, and then the treatment oriented group work with children.

Pre-Group Planning

As part of the pre-group planning the worker will prepare a complete blueprint of the work plan with the following details:

- The type of children
- Objectives
- The location
- Number and size
- Long-term or short-term
- Time schedule of group sessions
- Details of programme planning
- Resources needed including staff requirement
- Monitoring and supervision details, etc.

If the decision is being taken by an organization such as an NGO or a school, it should be discussed by all concerned and approved. A record of the meeting should be kept for future use. The discussion on each aspect will help in sorting out the details about the location, programme planning and resources, etc. It is obvious that some of these details would be finalized in consultation with the group/s. The next part of pre-group planning is to share the idea with the target clients.

Selection and Group Composition

The selection of members is done depending on the purpose of the group. In order to take a decision about forming the group, some facts about the children should first be collected. The criteria for selection of children, in case of groups of normal children are, the age group compatibility and sex compatibility. In some cases the class or caste aspect may also have to be kept in mind. However, the concept of balancing the role model is useful in selection of group members. A group with too many aggressive children will find it difficult to carry on smoothly, as will be the case with all slow learners in a group.

Consideration of physical characteristics, intelligence, general background such as state or regional affiliations, linguistic abilities, etc., can also help in the assessment of compatibility of group members. A question often asked is, should the selection be preplanned or should the group undergo changes as it progresses. Both options can be used. Considering the Indian situation it may be more pragmatic to start the group and make changes later as things become clearer. But a more professional approach will assess each member before the start of the group to determine their suitability.

As with other aspects of groups, there is virtually no sound research on preferred ways of selecting and composing a group for the children. During this period of development, except the more mature ones, children rely heavily on adults or older siblings as their model(s). For this reason, the group worker has more direct control over a group of children than over other age groups. Nevertheless, careful selection and grouping for maximum positive mutual influence is still of prime importance in forming treatment groups.

Although proper group composition is more important in treatment groups, the method of activity-interview group counselling has hardly been used in Indian conditions. The activity interview group counselling refers to the process where children are first put in an activity group where their behaviour is observed. They are then interviewed and selected for a group counselling session. The best predictor of the performance or functioning of a child in a group is some of the observed behaviour during a preliminary group placement. The child can be placed in an oversized newly formed group for a trial period of three or four sessions. The best participant combinations, based on direct observation of interaction, can be retained for the duration of the group. The others can be continued in open-ended group without therapeutic objectives.

The social age and the intellectual age of the group members must also be considered in the composition of a group. Some younger children who are overly aggressive and require the control of older group members are often deliberately placed in a group with older children. Similarly, some chronologically older but immature children are sometimes placed in groups with younger children. Generally, siblings and close relatives and friends should not be placed in the same group. When siblings are present in the same group, they sometimes feel compelled to look after each other thus reducing the possibility of independent participation. Also, there is a greater possibility of one telling on another, especially when angered or hurt in a family quarrel. The presence of close friends and/or relatives, poses the problem of trying to maintain an image. This image-maintenance behaviour interferes with the child's freedom to be real and spontaneous.

The following suggestions are given as guidelines for selecting children for group activities including where the group has therapeutic objectives:

1. In an open-ended group the worker can replace children who are not able to get along well. The concept of role balancing is useful as a rule of thumb to follow. Avoid overloading a group with a particular behaviour type, such as aggressive or hyperactive children.
2. Age and sex constitute two additional variables that the group worker must consider when composing a group for play. Small children below the age of ten can play in mixed sex groups, whereas older school-age children should be separated by sexes. For the most part, children of the same age constitute the best grouping. Exceptions are made deliberately to place more aggressive children in older age groups and some immature children in groups with children who are younger than themselves but not immature. A general practice to follow would be to compose groups with a year's difference in the chronological age.
3. Differences in caste, religion, and intelligence do not pose serious problems for young children. However, grouping those with gross differences in intelligence, such as inclusion of retarded youngsters with those of average to better than average intellectual ability, should be avoided.
4. Children unsuitable for children's group are children who as infants were deprived of close contacts with other children, children with murderous attitudes toward their siblings, children who have been exposed to sexual experiences, those who habitually steal, extremely aggressive children, and children who suffer from severe or acute trauma.

Group Size

The size of a group of young children, composed for the purpose of children's group, should be considered in the light of the need for careful observation and control. Young children usually are not good at listening while others are talking, taking turns, or being considerate of others who may be weak. In addition to lacking social controls, young children lack adequate control for their own and others' safety. The worker must therefore be alert to the safety needs of each child. To focus intently on what each child is attempting to communicate, requires eternal vigilance on the part of the worker. Since young children depend on their play and nonverbal means for much of their communication, the worker must control the number to monitor each child in the group and the group as a whole. In a large group, there are fewer opportunities for the development of close, intimate relationships among the children. Similarly, the worker will find it difficult to attend to every child's need. Therefore, the larger the number, the slower the development of group cohesiveness, which is critical in the development of a growth group. Among young children, cohesiveness is especially difficult to achieve, since each child is generally self-centred.

Another factor that could increase or delimit the worker's control is the nature of the children in the group. Although this problem should be controlled through role balancing, one or two rather aggressive and/or hyperactive youngsters in a group would necessitate more worker vigilance and control than a group of less aggressive or hyperactive children. When the preceding considerations are given to group size, a good practice is not to exceed ten, regardless of experience and competence.

Frequency, Length, and Duration of Group Sessions

All groups of children are generally growth oriented in India. The capacity building objective is oriented towards developing adequate behaviours to master successfully a given developmental task. It is remedial in the sense that a child is being helped to develop appropriate coping behaviours for facing certain stressful situations, learning to handle feelings and learn self-control. The growth-oriented group work with normal children does not require long-term interventions. Group sessions are generally an hour to two hour long and can be held two to three times a week for three to six months. In some cases the recreation groups can be made self-sufficient and can learn to function without the worker. Group work with normal children in recreation groups usually do not require intensive supervision, as is the case with children in treatment groups.

Combined with a supportive life skills training programme, group counselling could be effective on a forty-minute to one-hour-a-week basis, over a period ranging from three to twelve months. Children's group counselling that is primarily remedial, requires greater intensity of supervision, hence the length and frequency of group sessions is usually greater. Therefore, two group sessions of forty to sixty minutes in a week, are recommended.

The overall duration of group interventions is difficult to predict; however, periodic evaluation should be made with parents, teachers, and significant others, to appraise a child's progress. Usually, too much is expected by teachers, parents, and even workers. No minimum time can be set for remedial objectives in children's groups, but the worker should consider six months a reasonable period. At least three months should be allowed for any children's group. For those children who may be able to set their own goals, the time required for meeting their goals would generally depend on their own efforts in the group.

Planning the Activities

The most significant mode of communication in children is often non verbal and is usually loaded with feelings and actions (Dwivedi, 2005). Programme activities provide children an opportunity to engage in action, and are thus effective in helping them to express their feelings. The opportunity itself has therapeutic potential. It is useful to collect information about activities already in use and the outcome of these activities. Keeping a record of activities found interesting by children, would be useful. It is often seen that while initiating work with groups, the new workers/leaders do not pay enough attention to these facts. As a result, they are likely to select programmes and activities through a trial and error method, which is not a professional way of doing things. An effort to identify organizations working with children and holding discussions with them, can be a useful way of collecting facts about programmes and activities and children's responses to them.

Recreational activities have been a common feature of working with groups of small children. There are three factors in a group, which impact children (1) activities; (2) interaction with other children; and (3) the worker. Activities facilitate interaction in the group. Play activities, in particular, provide an opportunity for children to express their feelings and exhibit behaviour, which is frank and a true expression of what is lying dormant inside.

Amster (1943) has listed six uses of play:

1. Play can be used for diagnostic understanding of the child ... "we can observe the child's capacity to relate himself to others, his distractibility, his rigidity, his areas of preoccupation, his areas of inhibition, the direction of his aggression, his perception of people, his wishes, and his perception of himself. In the play, his behaviour, ideas, feelings, and expressions help our understanding of his problem and how he sees it".
2. Play can be used to establish a working relationship. This use of play is helpful with the young child who lacks the adult's facility for verbal self-expression, and with the older child who shows resistance or inability to articulate.
3. Play can be used to break through a child's way of playing in his daily life and his defenses against anxiety.
4. Play can be used to help a child verbalize certain conscious material and associated feelings.
5. Play can be used to help a child act out unconscious material and to relieve the accompanying tension. This cathartic use of play deals with symbolic material, which has dangerous significance to the child.
6. Play can be used to develop a child's interests, which he can carry over into his daily life, and which will strengthen him for his future life. This use of play has particular importance because of the correlation between the play and the work capacities of an individual.

As children have limited life experiences and have limitations in cognitive and emotional maturation, the group environment provides various opportunities for testing out realities. In an atmosphere of security, curiosity, interest and care, children may be able to correct their defective sense of reality. Gradually, children are able to move from egocentric, solitary and exploratory levels to more social, representational and constructive play activities, expressing their conscious and unconscious needs, thoughts feelings and conflicts (Dwivedi, 2005). It is time for the worker to change to social play activities, mimes, plays and skits, etc. Some other activities found useful are, singing, story telling, working with clay, and collage work. Always chose activities in consultation with children, or rather let them decide and make a schedule of activities to be conducted. They should then be encouraged to make the necessary preparation to procure material and other resources.

Educational Activities

This model of group work is somewhat unique in India. It aims at providing educational inputs to children who have never been to school, or are early drop outs. Such groups may have about 15-20 members, who are later divided into smaller groups. Providing education through non formal methods is one of the objectives of working with such children for social workers working in deprived communities. In groups where the purpose is to help the children to get some educational inputs to either mainstream them in school, or help them to become literate to function more effectively, the children should be identified on the basis of their educational needs. These children should then be assessed about their current educational abilities. Small groups should be formed based on the educational assessment. Each group should then be assigned an hour, three to five days a week, depending on the resources and time frame work evolved to achieve a particular level of education. The services of trained teachers should be used to provide educational inputs while the assessment of individual progress and general functioning of the group should be done by social workers with the help of the teacher/s. Small groups can be merged to hold sessions to discuss common inputs about the functioning of the group. Monthly progress reports are helpful in monitoring both achievement of individuals and group objectives.

The purpose of organizing educational activities, however, is not only to provide schooling. Informal education includes skill training in arts and crafts, training in life skill education, general awareness about social issues including drug and alcohol abuse, smoking and in general, health awareness. These activities are generally aimed at making children aware of the dos and don'ts, and using group influence to structure the change in attitudes and thinking. The activities should be carefully planned by the worker to generate discussion and action on the issues. The idea is not to simply give information but to create an impact on the consciousness of children. The group is used as a medium to help them reflect rather than follow instructions without understanding. The bonding in the group is used to strengthen the resolve. The participation by children in rallies, exhibition, paintings and poster designing gives them a sense of participation in tackling these issues in general, and taking a personal stand as well. The programme media skills of social workers is fully utilized while imparting informal education in groups.

Group Discussion

Group discussion is another activity which should be planned along with programme activities. The group should plan the sessions for group meetings in advance. The group functioning commences with the effort on the part of members to learn to think as a group rather than as an individual. Group discussion is used as a technique to develop democratic norms. It also helps the children to understand the need for taking decisions as a group. The group for example, should be made to realize the simple task of following the time schedule to facilitate smooth organization of activities. It is often seen that if this is not done, children turn up at different times and the programme sessions get delayed. Helping children to respect the time is a step in helping them to get more organized in life and to learn to think about others and as a group. Street children are known to be more informal in their approach to the group meetings. This is also an indicator of how much importance they attach to the meeting. The worker should make a note of these behaviours and analyze them as well. In India workers are not very meticulous about planning group meetings. The agenda is often not worked out and if it is worked out, it is not done in a participatory manner. The children thus may not be aware of the purpose of the meeting and the role they are expected to play. The worker generally does all the talking in the meeting. This may be necessary in the beginning but gradually the children or leaders in particular should be helped to take over the role of conducting the meetings. The purpose of the meetings generally is to discuss the following matters:

1. To assess the general functioning of the group activities, in particular developing and following group norms and schedules;
2. To assess the participation level of members;
3. To assess if the activities are meeting the individual and group needs; and
4. To assess the resources and their use, etc.

The First Stage or the Group Begins

The first session generally begins with an introduction by the worker or the group leader explaining the purpose and other relevant facts about the formation of the group. In dealing with the children in difficult circumstances the group leader will not begin by introduction of children, as the children know each other well. However, the worker can make an opening statement, "I am sure all the group members know each other very well. However if there is any one who does not know any member s/he may raise his/her hand."

It should be made clear right in the beginning that the group will manage all its activities and take its decisions. They will also be collectively responsible for all consequences of their overall activities in the group. This will serve as the contract, since no formal contract is signed in India between the clients and the worker. The first impression of children about the worker is very important although it is possible that they had already formed some opinion about the worker during the pre-group meetings. But, the way the worker explains the objective of group and the way s/he deals with group members, should further convince them of the professional competence of the worker. The opening statement of the worker about the purpose of the group and its participatory character is therefore extremely important, and should be prepared well in advance.

In the beginning phase, generally, an atmosphere of uncertainty prevails in the group. However, since children are far more flexible than adults, they are expected to settle down fairly easily, and are far more ready to experiment. They have some very definite ideas about what their needs are and how they want them to be met, yet they are also open to suggestions. The prior experience of children of working in a group is likely to vary. Street and working children have very different needs. Similarly institutional children have more specific concerns of coping with living conditions in an institution. They may have learnt not to trust anyone, and hence are likely to exhibit the same attitude towards the worker/leader. There is likely to be conflict among them for assuming the leadership roles within the group. Children in many contexts generally know each other and they carry their existing relationships to the group. At this stage therefore, it is important for the worker/leader to assess the degree of hostility/ compatibility in the group. No pre-session interviews with these children are needed but individual meetings to explain the purpose of the group and what is expected of them, is helpful. It is also very helpful to prepare a profile of each child highlighting their early history, and making a note of any personality characteristic needing special attention during group sessions.

The Middle Stage

Once a beginning has been made and programme activities are running as per schedule, it is time to make an assessment of the work. As suggested earlier, depending upon the time duration for the intervention, the time for assessment should be decided. This should however not be confused with the regular monitoring activity which is planned to collect information about activities on a more frequent basis. As a process, assessment involves gathering, organizing and making judgments about information. As a product, assessment is a verbal or written statement of evaluation about functioning of the group and its members, which is helpful in planning further action (Toseland and Rivas, 2001). Toseland and Rivas also indicate that the term diagnosis is also used by many authors in place of assessment, as also the fact that some authors avoid using either term, since they fear that by doing so they may be focusing more on the problem rather than the strengths or achievements. It is important to note that the purpose is to assess the situation to take corrective action to achieve group goals, for example, to assess the participation level of children and the interaction pattern in the group. Detailed observations of members' feelings and the changes in interest levels are helpful in assessment of progress of the group. The emergence of subgroups and the changes and influences on the internal dynamics of the groups should be noted. An analysis of group activities in terms of generating interest and actions is more helpful than simply mentioning the fact that the attendance is poor. The socio-cultural biases of workers can create problems in interpreting children's behaviour belonging to a different culture/social milieu, for example street children. This can be avoided by continuously rethinking the observations and interpretations. The other difficulty in assessment may arise on account of social workers being trained to assess individual behaviour in the context of the economic, social, cultural and psychological factors. However, while assessing behaviour in the group, the group context should be given due weightage along with other factors. The individual behaviour should be seen as an individual response to others in the group and as a process of interaction between members in a group. The two are very different ways of looking at the same reality. It is common in group records, for example, to see that the behaviour of a child is labeled but the statement of the child is not recorded, nor an analysis of the tone, to whom the remark was addressed and who responded, and how it affected the overall discussion. An assessment of the processes is more helpful than describing the end result while assessing the group functioning. The assessment in groups is more complex, as Toseland and Rivas (2001) pointed out, since it involves not only an assessment of individual behaviour but that of the dynamics of the group. The assessment should help the worker in understanding whether the group environment is facilitating the group functioning or creating problems. Assessment should be seen as a continuous process rather than a one-time exercise. As information is collected at regular intervals, it can reveal the changes and shifts in relationships. As many sources as possible for gathering information should be used for assessment purposes. The workers account of what happened in the group should be supplemented by member's self-appraisal of the happenings in the group. As a general guideline the worker should make an assessment about the general atmosphere in the group. Does it appear to be hostile-friendly; chaotic or disorganized-orderly and focused; inhibitive-permissive; formal-informal; and so on. An assessment of work being accomplished during a session in the group is also helpful. This concept of work assessment will vary as the group may be involved in play, education, discussion about problem solving and so on. The general assessment should indicate whether the group is making suitable progress or is just going around in circles being unclear about its goals, and the reasons for it.

It is important to assess the role of leaders in the group too. Assessment should focus on the individuals who are providing leadership to the group and the process of their emergence as leaders. A description of their leadership style and its impact on the group is also helpful. An assessment of how attentive they are to the needs of the group and whether both task and emotional needs are being looked after, should also be made. Another important aspect of assessment of groups is the participation level of children. It is important to determine whether the children are participating freely and enjoying being in the group or are they facing difficulties, as some children are more active than others. The capacity of children for participation needs to be carefully assessed. As indicated earlier, the assessment of participation related information based on several sessions will be more reliable than those based on a single session.

It is natural to assess how far the children are clear about the group purpose. An impressionistic understanding of the worker that all children know the purpose, may be misleading. Children have a tendency to forget and they may not be very focused on details. It may be worthwhile to keep assessing at different times the clarity about group purpose, as it helps in focusing their efforts for achieving the group goals.

An assessment of how stable the group has become is essential. Stabilization of members requires looking into individual members' interest level, and a clarity of what needs are being met through the group. In working with street children particularly, this needs special attention. Children living on streets lose hope. They are living a very difficult life full of struggles to survive on a day to day basis. They lose faith in the people and institutions around them, as generally with few exceptions, they experience exploitation and abuse. Female children undergo even tougher struggles to survive, as even fellow street children may handle them roughly. Both male and female children are abused physically, mentally and sexually all the time. Any efforts to win their trust and faith in the group activities will take a much longer time. They will not be very positive about the possibilities or help that the group can possibly offer to meet their needs. The stabilization of membership is important in India, as generally group work with children in many settings, including institutional children is planned on a long-term intervention basis. It is expected to last even after the withdrawal of the worker, in some cases on a self-sustaining basis. The worker should also need to know to what extent the group norms regarding the functioning of the group, particularly about meeting place, membership, programmes, leadership and other activities providing stability to the group, have been evolved. This is needed for the worker to plan a phased withdrawal from the group.

The Withdrawal Phase or Termination Phase

As stated earlier, the next phase is to give a finishing touch to the group activities. If the goals are short term, like in the case of recreation or growth groups including educational groups planned for a specific period, the worker will, after a proper assessment of the group's functioning, carry out an evaluation. Generally, in India, the major objective in working with children is to bring about growth in their personal capacities to deal with different situations. The evaluation therefore will assess to what extent the group activities and programmes have succeeded in providing the growth and change opportunities to the children. The changes in the attitude, thinking and behaviour of children should be evaluated through appropriate tools. The attitudes towards group members, peers outside the group, particularly those belonging to different cultures, family, community, the social worker and the sponsoring organization, should be covered. The worker in the evaluation refers specifically to children needing further support or interventions and specifies problem areas that still remain and how they should be handled in future. In group interventions where the worker's task is to get the group going and conduct activities like education or skill training etc., by employing other professionals, the evaluation will be with reference to the task at hand. The evaluation may result in the decision to extend the group activities or bring it to a close. In self-help groups of children, for example in case of street children, the evaluation should focus on:

- Clarity of the purpose
- Stability of membership
- Organizational structure
- Group Cohesiveness
- Group Norms

Sharing the Evaluation

The evaluation should be shared with the members of the group to help them realize what goals have been achieved. The members should be briefed in detail about how each member contributed to the success of the group functioning and what individual changes have occurred. The future need areas or goals should be explained. Referrals to concerned organizations if need be, should also be arranged. A summarized record of the group functioning and evaluation should be prepared and submitted to the sponsoring organization. The worker should keep a copy for personal use as well.

Group Work with Youths

The group work offers a lot of possibilities for working with young persons in the age group of 15 to 25 years of age group. This is a very formative age when individuals experience changes physically, psychologically and socially. There are very wide variations in the socio-economic situations of young persons in India. While a small section in the urban areas is experiencing a number of new facilities and services to be able to develop themselves, others are not only not able to do so but are suffering from grave deprivation of the basic facilities for education, recreation, health, employment and housing. The group work with young persons in rural areas and urban slums offer a very challenging task to social workers.

Objectives

The broad objectives of working with youth can be described as:

- The personal development;
- Providing support and guidance;
- Developing educational and vocational skills;
- Community and social action; and
- Problem-solving

The process of working with groups of youth will be same as discussed in the chapter on process. However, the process of youth group formation is somewhat easier as they are eager to experiment with any new activity, particularly the recreational and sports programme. The group aiming at behaviour modification of any kind including drug or alcohol related problems, would have to be formed with due care as discussed earlier in group counselling. Interviewing potential members prior to group formation will be helpful. Organizations working with young persons have focused more on recreation, education and vocational skill training programmes, and mobilizing youth for community or political activities. The group work with youth can have both short – and long-term objectives.

Locating Group Work with Young Persons

The possible places where social workers can locate the group work interventions will depend on the kind of client group they want to work with. A large number of urban young persons are located in schools and colleges. The worker can easily contact them through the college authorities. The workers can design the intervention giving details of objectives, programme activities, expected outcomes, evaluation process, time frame and cost, and make a presentation for the students and the college authorities. More informal discussions can be taken up later, to clarify any doubts or to provide details about the programmes and procedures. A two week camp for youngsters can be very helpful in starting a process of rediscovering the self and designing better strategies for meeting career goals, modifying self images, developing life skills, sensitizing youngsters about HIV/AIDS, drug abuse or violence and any other need area.

Out-of-School Young Persons

There are a large number of out of school young persons in India. These young persons can be located in the deprived communities and in rural areas. They have sufficient time at their disposal. They can be contacted by informal visits to the communities and through the non governmental organizations working in these communities, or by spreading information through posters, organizing sports and cultural activities and addressing community groups informally.

Young Persons in Residential Institutes

A large number of young persons are placed in reform institutions for varying durations. Group work with these persons can help in achieving the desired objectives of mainstreaming them in society. Developing better skills and attitudes, meeting recreation needs, fighting depression and aggression are some of the objectives that can be the focus of group work in this setting.

Personal Development

Most groups aimed at personal development of youth as also children, use recreational activities as programme inputs. The idea is to engage youth during their leisure time, to organize all kind of recreational programmes. Sport and physical activity programs can have a positive impact on young people's behaviour, and may provide an important vehicle for their personal development. Though the major group objective is projected as providing recreational activities but the group work objective is taken as growth and development of individual members. The worker helps the group to evolve norms for decision-making, encouraging wider participation of members in decision-making, developing a sense of fair play and respecting minority opinions. The activity based counselling model can be effectively used to focus upon the values and behavioural outcomes for modifying these.

Theatre including skits, street plays, group songs, poster making are some of the other activities with a lot of potential for improving communication, helping young persons to unburden themselves and learn to act as a team.

Educational Groups: In educational groups the main focus of the group activities is to pursue some educational objectives. Informal education through groups, helping young persons who are slow learners, out of school youth being helped to continue their education or skill training, are some popular uses of groups for educational purposes. Use of groups in educational camps is also commonly found in India. Helping young persons to acquire vocational skills to become self-employed through the process of group formation is a popular activity.

Support Groups: Support groups for young persons are generally formed to discuss problems being faced by them and to look for solutions. Young persons having drug-related problems, adolescents having emotional problems, unemployed young persons, all can be helped through support group activities. The major focus of support groups as stated earlier, is to provide a forum where persons with similar problems can come together, either as a self-help group or with relevant experts, to discuss the common problems being faced by them and to look for ways to cope with these in a more personally satisfying and socially acceptable way.

Remedial Groups: Remedial groups are meant to use group interaction and programme activities to modify behavioural responses of members. School social workers, probation officers and social workers working in observation homes and other organizations dealing with young persons coming in conflict with law, are places where remedial group activities are commonly found.

Community and Social Action Groups

Groups of young persons can be formed to tackle community needs in both rural and urban communities. These groups can be exposed to social problems such as women empowerment, communal violence, corruption, child labour, bonded labour, alcoholism, drug use and many other issues in society. They can be trained to act as volunteers and decide as groups about their own stand on many of these issues. They can be encouraged to develop a wider network to initiate changes. Social workers can provide consultancy to social and political organizations to make use of groups to develop social and political awareness among young persons to tackle social and political problems.

Group Work with Elderly

Group activities with elderly are also being undertaken by many organizations working with them.

Support Group: Support groups for elderly persons are helpful in dealing with depression which is normal in old age. Loss of active life, and reduction in income, power and physical health, induces a sense of loneliness and depression. Support groups help in overcoming these feelings, and sharing in groups help, to reduce tension as well.

Recreational Groups: In day care centres of elderly people, recreation groups can be organized for recreational activities. These groups can act as a support group as well.

Health Groups: Groups can be used to provide information and bring attitudinal changes relating to health among the elderly in India.

The groups for elderly are usually found in urban areas only as in rural areas the institution of *chaupal* (community centre in villages) is a usual meeting place for the elderly. Alongside, the people in the age group of 60+ continue to work or are firmly integrated in the family life routine. In urban areas, many people in this age group have more time on their hand and are usually looking for a place to meet other people. The old age day care centres that are being run by NGOs in some cities are places where group for the elderly can be formed for any of the above objectives. Forming a group of elderly is comparatively easier, as they are keen to participate in any activity where they can spend some time in a meaningful way. The participation in group activity gives them a sense of purpose to use their energies creatively. They feel welcome and if the group environment is healthy and creative they can do a lot of things that will meet their own needs and are helpful to others in the community.

Formation Stage

The worker explains the idea of the group and its purpose to the potential members individually. The worker then can call a meeting of potential members to discuss the idea in detail. The process activities are same and the worker should plan the meeting as explained in the process of working with group.

Middle Stage

Once the group settles down it should be helped to start planning its own activities. The worker can feed ideas to them as per the interest and socio-economic background of the group. The membership should be kept open and size is not a big problem in this case. However, if the number becomes too large more groups could be formed.

Monitoring and evaluation should be a planned activity at this stage to assess how stable the group has become, and how soon active involvement of the worker could be replaced by a less active monitoring role only. The other important thing to monitor is the activity level and leadership development in the group. The elderly people are capable of taking to leadership roles easily and as such, groups can get stabilized soon. The main problem is to get enough members enrolled so that the meetings become regular and can continue despite absenteeism. Rotation and diversifying activities and finding enough resources to keep the meeting place nice and comfortable is necessary to keep the group going.

Termination Stage

If the purpose of the group is short term, for example, to provide health related information or any other such short term intervention, the group can be prepared to end its activities. However, if the group is formed to continue on a long-term basis, the worker prepares for his/her withdrawal after transferring the leadership role to the members in the group. The worker makes it known to the members that the group has attained self functioning level, and it should continue. The worker also prepares some members to take over the activities s/he was carrying out. A helpline can also be provided to them in case of any specific help they may need.

If the sponsoring organization is running more than one group, a networking of all groups can also be worked out to provide another mechanism for keeping the groups active and become self sustaining. If need be, relevant legal procedures can be followed to link them with grant giving organizations for providing continuous financial support to the groups.

10

Group Work with Women

One of the recent developments in group work in India can be identified as the formation of self-help groups (SHGs) of women in different parts of the country. These groups are being formed in urban areas, in rural areas and in tribal areas as well. According to a recent study (Srivastava, 2004), nearly 25,000 SHGs all over the country were reported to be receiving finance from banks during the year 2002-03. This figure is only referring to SHGs generally formed by non-governmental organizations (NGOs) or those formed under government programmes by government workers specifically for the purpose of generating savings and using these groups as a source for financing their day-to-day needs. These groups, as we shall discuss in greater detail later on, are formed as a primary strategy for their economic uplift and for freeing them from the clutches of local money lenders. However, a number of organizations are forming groups of women which are focusing upon a variety of objectives which are not covered in the figures provided by the study. The fact is that using groups for the general empowerment or development of women has in recent times become a very popular group work activity in India. Yet, while looking at the study referred to earlier and other studies (see Meenai, 2003), it is clear that not much attention has been paid by researchers to study the whole field of working with groups of women in India. In this chapter we will attempt to highlight the various aspects of working with groups of women.

Groups of Women

Women have been making use of groups since a very long time for a variety of reasons in India. It is common to see groups of women coming together both in rural and urban neighbourhoods to use their leisure time in sharing information about life in general. These groups have acted as forums for recreation, social education regarding ceremonies and rituals to be observed on different occasions for example birth, marriages or deaths and religious festivals, for health education including sex education and so on. The groups have also performed therapeutic functions by acting as support systems to women, who unburden themselves by sharing their problems of all kinds in such groups. These groups have also at times acted as mechanisms of social control as they had power to impose sanctions if people deviated from social norms. The groups acted as sources of spreading information or disinformation in the larger community as well, at times unleashing wider social action unwittingly.

In rural areas in particular women found security in numbers as they had to face extremely difficult circumstances with no other mechanism available to provide them security. It is common knowledge that many women have to travel long distances in search of water, fodder, fuel or even toilet facilities, not available at home. They instinctively resort to go for meeting these needs in groups as they find security in numbers. It is commonly known as a number of studies have reported (see Jeffery, 1979; Kishwar et al., 1984; Jain, 1979), that women in India have very low self-esteem and as such lack self-confidence for facing any stressful situation alone. Not many women are comfortable in discussing their problems even with another woman individually. They respond better as a group. Talking to an unknown person of the other sex is still a very stressful situation for many young women. As a part of the socialization process itself women learn to rely on groups rather than facing a situation individually. The Indian cultural values, cutting across religious, caste and even class boundaries, are unanimous in keeping women more group oriented. A woman's psyche is specifically constructed to regard herself as secondary in comparison to the family's needs and in particular protecting its honour. Women are trained to be others oriented in all aspects of their lives, a trait which makes the group norms more important for them. A woman is therefore far more suited to becoming a stable member of a group than a male. However, her commitment to her family is far more important for her and her participation in other groups is considered secondary and at times forbidden if it conflicts with her family interests. A group has far more power over women than it has over males (See Cooper, 1979; Eagly, 1978).

Objectives of Group Work with Women

As we stated earlier, working with women through SHGs is of recent origin. In fact the centrestaging of women empowerment efforts in India is generally seen as a late seventies or early eighties' development during the twentieth century. Since the very definition of empowerment poses difficulties and is still being vigorously debated in India, many government programmes found it more convenient to focus on some long felt needs of women's development. Prominent among these were education, health and economic empowerment of women, both rural and urban. These, therefore, emerged as the main focus of group work objectives with women in India. The Mahila Samakhya and Swastha Sangh are two governmental programmes designed to use groups of women for promoting education and health respectively. The very concept of self-help refers to making these groups as sustainable as possible to serve the needs of women. This, in a sense, provides a unique example of group work of long-term nature, which is losing ground in group work practice in the west. The SHGs are seen as a vehicle of economic development in India, which though accepted as an objective in the literature on group work in the west, has in practice seldom been used as such. Group work with women in India, therefore, falls broadly in the task oriented model of group work, and in some cases as we shall see, may also address growth oriented goals. As an NGO described it, the main thrust of the group work with women in India is to help them learn to participate in decisions, which affect their lives. The SHGs of women have become very effective to accomplish a wide variety of objectives. These groups address such goals as: savings and income generation, providing support in emergencies such as violence at home or work place, etc. Besides these, the general group work objectives in working with women are:

Educational

Providing education to women on different aspects concerning their life, beginning from literacy skills to legal aid through the use of group work activities, is becoming a popular activity with many NGOs. Women of all ages, rural or urban, and belonging to different socio-economic groups, regions and religions, are participating in such groups. The nature of such group interventions is generally short term and task oriented.

Support

Support groups are meant to develop a network of women facing domestic violence and abuse both at home and at work place, or any other emotional problem, with the expressed purpose of empowering these women to confront the situation rather than remaining silent. Such groups, besides providing a forum for women to share their experiences and receive emotional support, have also been active in advocacy and social action. Support groups of women sex workers and women suffering from HIV/AIDS, are also being formed to help such women. Such group interventions are more long-term, where an attempt is made to stabilize these groups.

Livelihood

One of the most common objectives of groups of women is to attempt their economic empowerment. A number of self-help groups are being organized for helping them to learn to save, and to create a source for getting financial help from a more friendly and non-exploitative source. Women are also being helped to acquire economic skills of different kinds to augment their incomes through the use of groups.

Legal Aid

Some organizations are using groups to work with women to provide them legal aid concerning marital problems, inheritance matters, sexual harassment and any other aspect concerning their life. The nature of such group interventions may involve group counselling and acting as support network during legal battles to secure justice for members, besides undertaking educational and information sharing activities.

Health Groups

Use of groups for providing health-related information to expecting mothers, mothers with newly born babies or women suffering from various ailments including HIV/AIDS, is also being used by a variety of professionals in India. Besides providing information, the groups are also being used for inducing behavioural changes or attitudinal changes among women.

Formation Stage

One of the many questions that a worker is faced with is, "How do I form a group of women? Where do I begin? What am I supposed to do?" According to the process of group work discussed earlier the pre-group formation stage activity refers to contacting potential members individually or in small groups to share with them the idea of forming a group. So far all groups in India are agency generated groups, since people themselves are not generally taking such initiatives in general. NGOs and government organizations on the other hand, have found working with groups of women a useful strategy to accomplish a number of objectives. As stated earlier, the worker in India therefore has to educate the members about the needs or issues that the group will address and how it is likely to benefit them. The worker generally meets the potential members for the first time. Many members have little or no experience of working in such groups specifically formed on purpose. The formation stage thus will require careful planning, as discussed earlier (see the chapter on Process of Working with Group).

The planning for forming the group in particular should focus on the following details:

The social context: An understanding of the community the women belong to, such as the religion, caste, cultural norms about women, i.e., social mobility, purdah, family size and type, gender relations, etc., is very useful. Collect details such as:

- Educational status of family and women including attitude of family towards women's education.
- Economic status and occupation, women's participation in work, attitude of family towards women's work participation.
- Geographical location – urban, rural, tribal.

- Availability of water and sanitary conditions.
- Demographic profile – age group, numbers, etc.
- Availability of health services, etc.

Collecting some information about these issues will help the worker to understand the social background of the potential members. The worker should know about the stratification system and the social structure, especially relations between males and females and among people in general, and how it is likely to impact the formation and later interaction in the group. The social norms of the community will reveal how the community will receive the idea of women forming a group and what activities would be welcome. What are the current roles allocated to women, what are the gender relations in the family, how free are the women to take a decision to participate in the group activities? The social background in general will also help in preparing for capacity building inputs needed to develop the necessary self confidence among women in the group activities. The economic and occupational status of the family will also help in understanding the primacy of economic needs and the role women are currently playing in the economic sphere.

A crucial issue at this stage is, how do we collect information about these issues? The use of participatory methods with the purpose of looking at the issues from the people's perspective, is generally recommended. The central idea is to avoid our biases in looking at the social reality of the women. They should be treated as equal partners and encouraged to express the perceptions of their needs, or the urgency of these needs, in their life. The group formation will take place if the women decide to join the group on their own rather than being pressurized by the worker or any other person to do so. In India, in their anxiety to follow a target or a logical frame work approach there is a tendency to use short cut methods. The process of opening a dialogue and helping women to start a process of rethinking or change is a time consuming process and as such should be conceptualized as a long-term intervention. Meenai (2003) suggests a six-month period for achieving the formation of a self-help group in rural areas. This period may vary as the conditions will differ from rural to urban and tribal areas as also according to the variance in educational and awareness levels. For example, it will take less time to form a group in Kerala than in Rajasthan for the simple reason of the difference in literacy levels alone. The experience of working with some self-help groups indicates that incentives are helpful in generating interest and thus in the formation of group. In Aizawl, a tribal area, two social work students placed in a community during their field work, succeeded in forming a self-help group of women, in nearly three months by making them aware of the government scheme of providing economic incentives to women's group.

Need assessment: The worker should also analyze the basic purpose of forming the group/s. It is helpful to do a need assessment to select goals the group would be interested in. Make sure that group goals are in conformity with the needs of the women. Many a times the general assumption is that the need is well known, for example the economic need. Yet, when the idea of a savings group is shared, not many women show interest. The season is simple. Savings groups are not planned in a way that is economically attractive for women to spend considerable time there while they have other pressing issues to deal with in the family. For example a savings group wanted a group of twenty women to save Rs. 20 per month. The group thus envisaged a saving of Rs. 4,800 in a year. It planned to give four loans of Rs. 1000 or eight loans of Rs. 500 in a year to its members. This scheme did not get a good response from the women for the simple reason that four out of twenty or even eight out of twenty meant long odds and a waiting period of one year. The terms of returning the loan were also not clear at the planning stage. Similarly, the idea of a group for the purpose of educating women also did not evoke a positive response. Education, in the given situation of women, is a very low priority issue or a non-issue, since it was not clear how education would benefit the women in their present situation of acute poverty. In both cases the women belonged to low socio-economic strata in an urban slum. However, it must be noted that forming a group of women in a hospital for providing health related information is easier since it addresses an immediate need of women and they have some time allocated for coming to the hospital or a health centre. Similarly, if a provision of incentive in the form of an equal amount being contributed by the bank or any other financial organization is made in case of a saving group, backed by some entrepreneur skill training and provision of financial help to start a small business, the group can become an attractive proposition.

Knowing about the social background of women in general will help the worker to deal with the prevailing social norms about women's participation. It will mean:

- Identifying and meeting the opinion leaders.
- Planning meetings with the families of women.
- Preparing the details of the proposed group activities such as objectives, programme and activities of the group, time schedule, meeting place and time, role of women, possible benefits to the family and community in general, etc.

In planning for formation of women's group, the worker must take in to account the role of the sponsoring organization as well i.e., what time frame the organization has prepared for the formation of group/s, actual number of groups to be formed, objectives to be achieved, number of staff and other resources assigned for the task, etc. The steps involved in planning a women's group thus are:

- Work out a time-table for formation of group.
- Collect information about community.
- Meet opinion leaders.
- Meet family members including women to share the idea of group formation.
- Meet the women to orient them about group formation.
- Organization of capacity building programme for women to cover the following topics: Introduction of sponsoring organization, group goals, interaction among members, leadership in groups, group decision-making, programmes and activities, record keeping in groups, procedural rules, group and community, women and development, etc.
- Finalize the number of groups to be formed and locations of the groups.
- Make a tentative list of members wanting to join a group in a participatory manner. Schedule a meeting of the group/s to work out the preliminary details about group objectives, frequency of meetings, place and time of meeting, allocation of roles to different members, for example, making one or two women responsible for making arrangements for the future meetings, keeping records of the meetings, etc.

- Prepare a list of workers and work out the details of how many groups a worker or a team of workers will work with.
- Identify the support staff needed for training or capacity building activities as also for other programmes and activities to be organized later in the group.
- List if collaboration from other institutions, such as education department, schools, health centres, banks or other financial institutions, is needed and where they are located.
- Establish contacts with these organizations to explore what help they are prepared to offer, and on what terms.

Once all these activities are carried out, the group formation stage will generally be completed. The success of formation stage is simple to assess. A good indicator is whether the women start taking interest in the group activities and start attending the group meetings on their own initiative without frequent reminders or persuasion. If the women are still not showing enough interest after first three or four meetings, the worker must do some rethinking about the group goals and objectives, time schedule, the place, social context and distance of group meetings, etc., in order to arrive at an understanding of women's lack of interest. The necessary modifications will have to be made to convince the potential members that the group is capable of meeting the felt needs of the members. Unless that is done the group will not get off the ground. It will remain an idea on the part of the worker or the sponsoring organization. It is also evident that this process of convincing can also be a gradual process. Women, in particular in rural areas with little or no education, will move at their own pace.

Middle Stage

The worker at this stage needs to consolidate the group activities and try and assess how things are going in the group, to make necessary modifications if need be, to achieve the group objectives. Even though the worker may be able to initially generate interest in the group activities, the interest can decline if proper planning to maintain it is not done. The monitoring process should commence along with an effort to develop effective leadership in the group.

Prepare a profile of potential members:

- Their educational status
- Their general awareness level of social issues

- Their self-confidence level
- Their communication skills
- Their health status in general terms
- Their general personality type or profile
- Their cultural inhibitions or value preferences

Develop a system of monitoring the progress of individuals and groups by evolving indicators of change.

For Members

Attendance	*Regular*	*Irregular*	*Absent*
Contribution to group	Good	Average	Poor
Group tasks	Good	Average	Poor
Interaction	Very social	Average	Isolate
Relating to worker	Good	Average	Poor
Relations with members	Very social	Average	Isolate
Others orientation	Good	Average	Poor
Trying to improve self	Good	Average	Poor
Helping others	Good	Average	Poor
Developing norms	Good	Average	Poor
Helping to enforce norms	Good	Average	Poor
Drawing out silent members	Good	Average	Poor
Communication skills	Good	Average	Poor
Others orientation	Excessive	Moderate	Poor
Expertise level needed by the group for task	Excellent	Good	Average
Emotional integration of group	Excellent	Good	Average
Leadership skills	Excellent	Good	Average

For Group

Meetings of Groups	*Very Frequent*	*Frequent*	*Infrequent*
Attendance	well attended	average	poor
Organization	well organized	average	poor
Interaction	warm	average	hostile
Leadership	effective	average	unfocussed
Task Accomplishment	good	average	poor
Programme and Activities	interesting	average	boring
Programme and Activities	interesting	need based	not focused catering to segmental needs

The data on all these indicators should be collected on a regular basis and analyzed periodically to assess the changes taking place or the progress of the group. The information on these indicators should be collected from members and leaders as well, to see the difference in perception or how different persons rate the group progress.

Based on these assessments identify potential leaders and training inputs for members as well.

The inputs at this stage will vary depending upon the objectives the group is focusing on. For example, the self-help groups for providing livelihood or economic benefits to women, are likely to be long-term interventions. Similarly groups formed to focus on women's empowerment will also be long-term interventions requiring considerable inputs during the middle phase, to consolidate the formation stage activities. The worker should assess the efforts made to sustain interest, develop group norms and structure, capacity building inputs for the members to function more efficiently in the group, development of leadership and linkages with other organizations, in order to facilitate the achievement of group goals.

In case of short term group interventions for working with pregnant women, adolescent girls, women suffering from HIV/AIDS and so on, the middle stage inputs would be, assessing how much progress has been achieved in providing necessary information, inputs, and achieving attitudinal changes, etc.

It may be relevant here to discuss how the task of defining the objectives is carried out in working with groups in general, and with women in particular. The organizations in general are adopting broad objectives such as women empowerment, poverty alleviation, enterprise development, awareness generation, improvement in health and education status, etc. However, a better approach is to be more specific and concrete in defining objectives, for example:

- At the end of the group intervention all group members must be literate.
- No group member is in debt.
- All pregnant women in the group have been immunized.
- All adolescent girls in the group have basic understanding of reproductive health.

- Women in the group have learned to open and operate an independent account in the post office/bank.
- All members in the group have attended a training programme in leadership skills.

These objectives can be checked at different times to see the progress made. Once these are achieved, the decision for terminating or diversifying the objectives can be taken.

Termination or Withdrawal Stage

In India, group work in many situations is planned as a long-term activity and thus one of the objectives is to make the group a self-sustaining activity or unit. The termination or ending is not the actual act. Instead it is a kind of withdrawal of the worker to enable the group members, including the leaders, to assume responsibility for many activities, which earlier were being carried out by the worker. However, in the Indian context, the stage of self-sufficiency is a long-term goal, which may take as long as three to five years. Even then a system of periodic monitoring should be put in place to make sure that the groups continue to function.

11

Self-Help Groups

Concept

Self-help groups (SHGs) have become the most popular form of group work that are being used by both governmental and non-governmental organizations in India to accomplish a variety of development goals in recent times. However, the idea of self-help was an inherent part of group work practice right from the very beginning. The migrants in settlement houses in United States, left to fend for themselves in the new environment, were encouraged to come together to solve the common problems facing them. As Konopka (1963) noted, "whereas philanthropy was generally of middle class origin, mutual self-help, as the name implies, developed from the need for mutual aid and support". Similarly, as Mayadas et al. (2004) noted, settlement movement – which lead to the birth of group work – was a social [collective] response to difficult social conditions, and relied on group [mutual help] to solve problems. The beginnings of collective bargaining to improve wages, as an effort to preserve cultural traditions, to promote adult education and to provide growth opportunities to their children through camping, were all initial attempts at using groups to tackle common problems through mutual help. The groups that emerged later on to acquire an international presence, such as Alcoholics Anonymous, were also based on the idea of self-help. The assumption in these kinds of groups was to bring together people facing similar problems, to provide support to each other, along with generating ideas to manage the problems. The experience sharing and the mutual support were seen as major helping factors in these groups.

As a document promoting a self-help group claimed, the objective of the group is to provide knowledge about how to receive help, give help and help yourself. Underlying self-help is the basic theme: *"You are not alone"*. Benefits to members are seen as:

- They feel less isolated knowing others share similar problems;
- Exchange ideas and discuss effective ways to cope with problems;
- Actively work on their attitudes and behaviour to make positive changes in their lives; and
- Gain a new sense of control over their lives.

The knowledge base of self-help mutual support groups is experiential, indigenous, and rooted in the wisdom that comes from struggling with problems in concrete shared ways. Self-help groups build on the strengths of their members.

Many of these groups have developed without using any professional group worker's help, but professionals may have facilitated some of these groups at some stage or other. Some of these groups thus become more or less self-reliant in handling their own affairs. However, the success story of some of these more well-known groups, should not make us think that self-help groups can easily be formed and sustained. Katz (1993) highlighted that the initial development of self-help groups is critical for understanding them and to work out what strategies would be more suitable to assist them in their development.

Wituk et al. (2003) suggests that three areas are critical to understand the self-help groups. They are:

1. Reasons for starting the self-help groups;
2. The steps and tasks involved in their development; and
3. The sources of satisfaction and frustrations.

They found in their study that people start self-help groups because they want to connect with others who share their concern. Many founders of the group said they started a group as they felt there was a need in the community. An important fact that emerged was that participants recognized that the self-help group was providing a kind of support, which other support systems such as family and church were not.

The method to start the group was informing various agencies like hospitals, churches, health departments and so on and giving ads in the newspapers, TV and radio about the group. Professionals were also requested to refer clients to the group.

The difficulties faced were generally in finding a suitable meeting place, lack of participation, leadership development, etc. The study did not analyze the actual purposes of the self-help groups, but it is clear that generally people facing some kind of problems came together to find support and learn from each other.

Uses of Self-Help Groups

The self-help groups can be formed for any number of objectives. However, the groups offering emotional support like the study indicated, are not very common in India. Some groups of sex workers, drug addicts and other persons facing problems have been formed by different organizations in India, but the number is not very large. The purpose again is not simply emotional support but economic strategies for survival or rehabilitation. Self-help groups of single mothers and abandoned women are also being formed in India to help these women. The use of self-help groups in India has been more popular to help women and to a lesser extent small farmers or agricultural workers and other deprived populations. The objective of these self-help groups has been to meet economics needs of the members. In case of some women's groups objectives such as awareness generation to improve self-concept, knowledge of laws and sources from where help can be obtained, are some additional ones. Some women's groups provide protection to their members and also other women in the community against domestic violence. There are some examples of the groups tackling social or community issues as well. In Sri Lanka and India, self-help groups of old people have been formed by international organizations such as Help Age, to bring older people together. The objective is to provide support to each other, share solutions to common problems and take economic decisions as well. In Kerala, an NGO has started self-help groups consisting of the elderly, children, and parents of mentally and physically challenged children as well. The purpose in the case of the elderly is providing mutual support to help them to fight depression, and help them with other problems. Children's groups are formed to promote scholastic abilities of children with mutual help and support.

The other notable feature in India has been of conceiving all types of social work interventions in a social welfare perspective, focusing on deprived populations only. Other segments of the populations like the economically well off but facing problems of social functioning, have generally been neglected as a target population needing professional help by social workers. This segment often experience stress, are unsure of their relationships, lack social skills and as such need a variety of services. Group work with working mothers facing role overload, sexual harassment, and depression, and children needing help in becoming focused in their studies or facing relationship problems at home or at school, has not been tried in India. Abuse of alcohol and drugs is affecting a sizable section of an upwardly growing population. Children from well-off families are showing symptoms of Attention Deficit Hyper Activity Disorder, resulting in problems at home and at school. Forming self-help groups of many such clients is a distinct possibility. Lesser et al. (2004) give the example of a group of professional middle aged women who have supported members in balancing career and family roles through transition and stressors in their work and family life.

The main objectives for forming self-help groups can therefore be summarized as follows:

- For meeting economic needs of the deprived populations
- For providing psycho-social support to members
- For dealing with community related problems

Planning Self-Help Groups

Once the worker or the leader initiating the group decides the general purpose for the formation of the group, the planning for formation of a self-help group shall begin. Meeting the economic needs of the poor is a major priority area. We shall therefore begin with such groups. The general nature of such groups in India is to help them develop a fund through savings and then provide loans to their members. Some groups help their members to start an income generating activity as well. The purpose is to enable groups to help the members to become self-sufficient in managing their economic needs, without relying on any exploitative sources such as money lenders. Many government programmes are providing economic inputs by way of subsidies, loans and technical inputs to help these groups to take up small business activities.

Despite the fact that the economic condition of the target population is well known, the other characteristics of the population such as education, economic skills, family size and household responsibilities, time schedule of daily routine, self-perceptions, cultural practices, etc., should be carefully studied. Initial pre group discussions with families rather than individuals should be held using participatory methods to assess their mental preparedness for the new experience.

The worker should work out the details of capacity building programme for the members, such as:

- Organizing literacy programmes;
- Sensitizing males about women's role and status in the society;
- Skill development; and
- Leadership development.

The preliminary details of the group functioning such as rules for joining the group, the size of the group, expected roles and responsibilities of members, and likely benefits, can also be discussed at the pre group discussion stage. The worker will have to work out these details in advance in conjunction with the group members.

Many schemes providing assistance to self-help groups provide details of the requirements that the groups should comply with [see for example the guidelines provided by Swarnjayanti Gramin Swarozgar Yojna Guidelines (Government of India, 1999)]. The guidelines suggests that:

1. A self-help group may consist of 10 to 20 persons. In the case of minor irrigation, and in the case of disabled persons, this number may be a minimum of five (5).
2. All members of the group should belong to families living below the poverty line. The group shall not consist of more than one member from the same family. A person should not be a member of more than one group.
3. The group should devise a code of conduct (Group Management Norms) to bind itself. This should be in the form of regular meetings (weekly or fortnightly), functioning in a democratic manner, allowing free exchange of views, and participation of the members in the decision-making process.
4. The group should be able to draw up an agenda for each meeting and take up discussions as per the agenda.
5. The members should build their corpus fund through regular saving. The members themselves should decide the quantum of

savings. The group should be able to collect the minimum voluntary savings. The group should be able to collect the minimum voluntary saving amount from all the members regularly. The savings so collected will be the group corpus fund.

6. The group corpus fund should be used to advance loans to the members. The group should develop financial management norms covering the loans sanction procedure, repayment schedule and interest rates.
7. The members in the group meetings should take all the loaning decisions through a participatory decision-making process.
8. The group should be able to scrutinize the loan applications, fix repayment schedules, fix appropriate rate of interest for loans advanced and closely monitor the repayment of the loan installments from the members getting loan.
9. The groups should operate a group account, so as to deposit the balance amounts left with the groups after disbursing loans to its members.
10. The group should maintain simple basic records such as Minutes Book, Attendance Register, Loan Ledger, General Ledger, Cashbook, Bank Passbook and Individual Passbooks.

The National Bank of Agriculture and Rural Development (NABARD) has developed a project of linking SHGs with the banks for their credit needs. The check list prepared by the organization to assess the loan worthiness of the SHG, provides a good guideline for the worker to ensure certain standards of SHGs formed for the purpose of meeting economic needs.

- SHGs with 12-16 very good factors can get loan from the bank immediately.
- SHGs with 10-12 very good factors need 3-6 month to improve before being considered for loan.
- SHGs with rating of less than 10 very good factors will not be considered for loan.

The banks can sanction a loan of up to four times the saving amount of the group. The loan is sanctioned to the group. The SHG can take a loan from the bank for any purpose such as emergency needs, illness in the family, marriage or purchasing assets for income generating, etc. (Nanda, 1995).

NABARD Checklist to Assess an SHG

S. No.	*Factor*	*Very Good*	*Good*	*Unsatisfactory*
1.	Group size	15-20	10-15	less than 10
2.	Type of members	Only very poor	2-3 not very poor	many not be very poor
3.	No. of meetings	4 in a month	2-3 in a month	less than 2
4.	Timing of meetings	night or after 6.00 pm	between 7 and 9 in the morning	other timings
5.	Attendance	more than 90%	70-90%	less than 70%
6.	Participation of members	Very high	medium	low
7.	Saving collection	4 times a month	3 times a month	less than 3 times
8.	Amount to be saved	fixed amount	varying amount	–
9.	Interest on internal loan	depends on purpose	24-36%	more than 36%
10.	Utilization of saving amount	fully used for loaning members	partly used for loaning members	poor utilization
11.	Loan recoveries	more than 90%	70-90%	less than 70%
12.	Maintenance of records	all books are regularly maintained and updated (minutes, maintaining saving books, records loan register)	only important books maintained and updated	Irregular in maintaining records
13.	Accumulated savings	more than 5000	3000-5000	less than 3,000
14.	Knowledge of the rules	known to all	–	not known to all
15.	Education level	more than 20% literate	–	less than 20% literate
16.	Knowledge of government programmes	all are aware	most are aware	no one knows

Source: (Nanda, 1995).

The worker can prepare a set of model rules for the group to discuss and finalize. Model rules for a self-help group are:

- Members will agree to abide by the rules.

- Only one member from a family will be enrolled as a member.
- The group will have a total of XX members.
- New members may be admitted if there is a vacancy.
- Members will elect a president to preside over the meeting for a year.
- Members will elect a secretary to correspond on behalf of the groups with other organizations for a year.
- Members will contribute a monthly amount as decided by the group.
- The amount collected will be kept in a bank.
- Member who fails to pay three consecutive instalments will lose his/her membership.
- Member will maintain his/her contribution book regularly.
- Members will attend meetings of the group regularly.
- Member will return the loan in 10 equal instalments.
- Member will pay an interest rate of 2 per cent on the loan.
- Group will decide the action to be taken against a member who fails to return the loan.

The worker can invite relevant experts from financial, training or other institutions to address pre group meetings for the purpose of providing clarity to potential members about the functioning of the group.

For example, one of the organizations helping women to form and run self-help groups have worked out its details as follows:

Objectives of Setting up and Supporting Self-Help Groups

1. To make the members economically self-sufficient.
2. To help farmers achieve sustainable development.
3. To protect the rights of farmers.
4. To use government resources for welfare of the farmers.
5. To look for marketing avenues for farmers.
6. To provide capacity building for food processing to farmers.
7. Capacity building for product design and product selection.
8. To motivate them for economic development.
9. To remove corruption.

10. To unite the poor families for development.
11. Help the youth find employment.

Requirement for Registration

- The group should have a name
- List of members with addresses
- The group should have a bank account
- Each member should have a pass book showing details of contributions made
- Rules and regulations of the group
- The list of office bearers
- Choice of trade

Grading of Group

- Duration of existence of SHG
- Periodicity of meetings
- Attendance records of meetings
- Minutes of the meeting
- Quality of financial administration
- Earnings so far and current bank balance
- Rate of interest charged from members
- Number of members given loan
- Pattern of repayments
- Members with expertise in any skill area
- Knowledge of group members about group goals

Another organization working with self-help groups of women has the following objectives:

- To bring empowerment through self-help concept, i.e. development through participation.
- To inculcate a habit of saving among the families.
- To decrease dependency on moneylenders.
- To enhance their confidence and skills.
- To increase awareness on various local institutions and schemes.
- To help develop micro enterprise.
- To initiate and implement community development activities.

Process of Formation of the Group

The process of formation of the group as indicated by Wituk et al. (2003), such as informing the people through the media and institutional arrangements, will not work in the case of poor persons in the Indian situation. The main difference lies in convincing the members about the usefulness of joining the group. In the west, people themselves decide to join a self-help group, whereas in India the worker motivates them to join. The worker has to put in a lot of effort for informing the community and clarifying their doubts about the need to join the group. Further, s/he has to make the group objectives attractive enough for them to join the group. Usually workers have been using short cuts in the formation process in their hurry to show results by enrolling members in groups, only to discover that they never turn up. It may be preferable to promote a number of groups as it will reduce the cost of capacity building programmes. Each individual in the group would not require the close personal attention of the worker besides periodic monitoring. The following steps will help in the process of helping people to form groups:

- Hold discussions in the community with a number of families and present all the details about the group as planned earlier.
- Visit influential leaders to inform them about the programme.
- Visit individual families to clarify their doubts.
- Hold specific discussions with male members if the groups are for women (see Process of Working with Women's Group).

The process of formation of a group should be left to the initiative of the people. It should be their own decision. They are expected to discuss and decide on their own to start a group, and also its objectives, size and other details of the membership. The worker can facilitate the process, by advising them about the size, amount of money they can collect as monthly contribution, how to open a bank account, how to elect their leaders, where to hold a meetings and so on.

Self-help groups broadly go through the following three stages of evolution:

1. Group formation (formation, development and strengthening of the groups to evolve into self-managed people's organizations at the grassroots level).

2. Capital formation through the revolving fund, and skill development (managerial skills for management of their organizations as well as the activity).
3. Taking up economic activity for income generation (Government of India, 1999).

As the document suggests, the stages in the life of a self-help group are purely economic in nature. However, Myrada, a non-governmental organization working with small groups suggests that in the initial stages women come together to socialize and spend time with each other. The objective of savings and credits are not their immediate priority (Fernandez, 1994). However, there are no set patterns. If the groups are specifically being formed for economic purposes, the group should be clear about it and start taking some action in respect of achieving these objectives. There are other studies which suggest that social mobilization should be seen in the wider context of achieving other goals as well, besides financial objectives, such as collective agency and support (Kay, 2002), particularly in the case of women's groups. This simply means adding more inputs such as health services, training in legal, social and political issues, etc.

The Middle Stage

The middle stage is crucial in stabilizing the group. The worker should monitor the actual inputs in the group by way of activities and its impact. Records of the number of meetings held, members' attendance, contributions received, etc., should be analyzed. A crucial activity to monitor is the financial administration of funds, for example, how many loan transactions are taking place and the repayment trends. At this stage, the focus should be on helping the group to carry out its routine activities regularly. In case of irregular meetings and attendance the leaders should be asked to make more efforts to regularize the routine. If this fails to make the group more regular the goals of the group and its functioning may be reviewed. The worker will have to ensure during the planning stage that goals of the group are attractive enough for the members. A process of capacity building should also be started at this stage in the following areas. This may be done by:

- Initiating capacity building;
- Starting literacy classes;

- Introducing legal, social and political awareness building programmes;
- Developing trade related skills;
- Conducting life skill training programmes; and
- Imparting financial skills.

The capacity building programmes for members will help in stabilizing the group. The goals of the group can be reviewed to make suitable changes. For example, the groups that started as saving groups can expand their goal to start income generation programmes. A women's group may add legal awareness or other activities as part of its goals. The worker should prepare a strategy to regularize the functioning of the group at the planning stage itself by anticipating the possible causes for lack of inadequate participation.

How attractive is the group goal?

Supposing a savings group is started with a membership of 20 and each member is expected to contribute Rs. 50 per month. It means the group will have an income of Rs. 1,000 per month or Rs. 12,000 per year. The group can start helping the members by giving loans of Rs. 2,000 after two months. In the beginning, only one member at a time can be helped. If a subsidy is likely to follow after the end of one year, it can be an additional incentive for the members and the group. Is the group goal attractive enough for members? There is no easy answer to this question; it will depend on the local poverty situation, members' income level and their expectations from the group. It is here that worker's analysis based on his/her pre group discussions with the potential members and the facts collected about the members socio-economic back ground will be helpful.

Work out details of income-generation activity

One of the main weaknesses of self-help groups formed for meeting economic needs, is their lack of clarity about their income generation activity and its outcome. There are a number of studies that have studied self-help groups and their impact on the members' economic and social development (see Indira and Rao, 2001; Bandhyopadhya, 2002; Devasa and Jancy, 2004). Almost all suggest that members have experienced an improvement on both fronts. The groups have undertaken economic activities such as poultry, animal husbandry, and have also been trying the traditional non farm activities such as petty shops, kirana shops, flower selling, candle making, masala and pickle making, making bamboo items, brass ware, khadi, leather goods and many other craft related activities. However, no details of cost inputs, profit margins, marketing skills and capital requirements etc., have been worked out in advance. Similarly, these details have to be region and area specific. This is one reason that a lot of uncertainty prevails about the economic outputs. It is not realized that even if some of these small activities succeed, the profits will not be adequate enough to make a very substantial improvement in the life of the families. Secondly, the success stories of some groups are considered as special efforts made by some very committed leaders, which are seen to be out of reach of the common people.

Another major problem is that the NGOs organizing these groups themselves do not possess enough economic expertise. The experience therefore suggests that working with self-help groups for meeting economic needs requires team work. The services of different professionals should be included in the plan for meeting economic needs. There are different options which the leader/worker should consider:

- Should the plan aim at developing an income generation activity for the entire group? If so, what should be the size of the group? What capital inputs would be needed to provide an adequate level of profit sufficient to meet the needs of the entire group?
- Should the plan attempt to help individual members to develop their own individual income generation activities? Should the group provide loan and training facilities for facilitating the individual activities? What system of repayment should be there and how many members should be provided help by the group at a time?

Another important point to consider is how many groups an organization should start at a time and the staff inputs needed to manage these. Auxiliary services that have reportedly been effective in enhancing and complementing micro-credit are business development services, business planning, marketing, accounting and technology (Kay, 2002).

Some general guidelines for starting income-generation activities are as follows:

- The income generation activities to be started should not be very capital intensive.
- The skill level for the activity should either be available in the group or can be developed with some training inputs.
- The demand, marketing, costing, pricing, design and quality of the product should be studied and worked out with the help of experts and should not be left to chance or a trial and error method.
- The financial requirements should be carefully worked out.
- Prepare a schedule of targets to be achieved by the group.

The Evaluation Phase

In this phase, as suggested in the chapter on process, an evaluation of the work done should be undertaken based on actual facts. The main thrust of evaluation is to assess the extent to which the objectives have been achieved. It should also provide the worker/leader an insight into the problems and any course correction to be carried out for future activities. The emotional integration of the members, the quality of their participation, the development of leadership and the level of sustainability achieved by the income generation activity, should be carefully evaluated. This will help the worker in discussing with the group the future time table of the worker's involvement with the group and to plan for the continuance or termination of the activity and the group. The experience of working with self-help groups in India suggests that self-sustainability without the NGO backup is difficult to achieve in Indian conditions. A minimum period of five years is necessary to develop the group to a level of comparative self-sustainability. Even then some kind of support network to periodically monitor and help the groups in continuing their activities will be needed. Developing efficient indigenous leaders is also helpful in attaining sustainability.

Some insights about the functioning of SHGs are provided by the following case study of SHGs done in the three states of Karnataka, Tamil Nadu and Andhra Pradesh by NABARD (1995), (Nanda, 1995).

1. An NGO took six months to one year for forming the groups. The process of evolution of SHG was found to be voluntary.

2. Source of funds to SHG was initially savings and NGO's contribution. Bank credit came later.
3. The share of loan for income generating activity increased from 22 per cent in the first year to 74 per cent in the third year.
4. Activities financed by the SHGs were need based and the SHGs were flexible in their approach.
5. The groups adopted a flexible approach in charging interest on loans ranging from 18 per cent to 36 per cent, but the interest was lower than the rate charged by money lenders.
6. Shorter repayment periods were fixed and the repayments were made from all available resources, i.e., by also including other income besides income from the activity financed through the SHG loan. The members were therefore able to take more than one loan in a year. The general opinion was that long periods of loan with grace years and infrequent loan installments, lead to overdues, as in the case of a formal credit delivery system.
7. Conducting regular weekly meetings was one of the hallmarks of effective functioning of the groups.
8. Income per member had registered a significant increase during the period of last three years of group formation.
9. Group formation helped the members in attending to individual and common problems more effectively.
10. Some SHGs have started creating common assets owned by all members. These common assets also provide additional income to the group.
11. Role of NGO/voluntary agency is important for group formation, sustenance of SHG, fund support, training and advice. The voluntary agency had also helped in providing necessary linkage for economic activities.
12. The bankers were concerned about sustainability of the groups in the long run. They were also concerned about the groups functioning in the event of withdrawal of the NGO.
13. The rate of interest charged was 3 per cent per month on the loans given out of the thrift amount and 1.10 per cent per month on loans given for income-generating activities under the linkage with a bank in Andhra Pradesh.
14. The voluntary agency plans to withdraw from the existing groups by creating an apex body in each of the areas it is operating. This

'apex body' was expected to provide umbrella support to the SHGs in the future in Tamil Nadu.

Let us look at some other studies of savings and credit groups and its impact on the members, particularly relating to empowerment of women and in particular the poor.

- The process of social mobilization needs to be accompanied and complemented by economic security. As long as the disadvantaged suffer from economic deprivation and livelihood insecurity, they will not be in a position to mobilize (UNDP, 2001).
- Increased self-confidence is especially pronounced when women are exposed to training on women's rights and social and political issues (Kay, 2002).
- The process of social mobilization should be conceptualized more broadly so that the groups can perform more encompassing roles. Institutional frameworks, which bring these groups together and harness their collective strengths, are also necessary. A promising example is the federating of self-help groups, where all such groups in one village form an apex body consisting of selected representatives of each group. Women leaders in federated bodies have gained prestige and recognition, which has paved their path to elected office in local government. These federated bodies can be linked further, reaching up to the national level, presenting opportunities for women to engage in decision-making, at higher levels. It is at the level of political decision-making that women can hope to have a voice in transforming society. In this regard, affirmative action, whereby women are allocated quotas in various decision-making bodies, can be an effective strategy. Examples are the reserved seats for women in the local tambon administrative organizations in Thailand and in the parliaments of Pakistan and Bangladesh (Kay, 2002).
- One important shortcoming is that as micro-credit is made available to groups based on collective collateral, the process of group formation often precludes the very poor, who are perceived as being poor credit risks (Krishnaraj and Kay, 2002).
- Micro-credit practitioners have often maintained that their first and highest priority is financial sustainability. Non-financial services were seen as adding costs and detracting from the main

aims of micro-credit. However, experience from several countries has shown that micro-credit can play a greater role in poverty and vulnerability reduction, when it is complemented by non-financial services. Among the ancillary services, one of the most useful would be health-related (Kay, 2002).

- The yardstick for measuring the performance of micro-credit schemes should not be based on economic variables such as loan repayment rates, alone. While financial viability is important for sustainability, indicators should also include the contribution to meeting basic needs for household subsistence, reducing vulnerability to risks and enhancing social capital and empowering women (Kay, 2002).

Self-Help Groups for Providing Psycho-Social Support to Members

Self-help groups for providing psycho-social support to persons facing such problems are not very common in India currently, but can be a useful strategy to provide help. The strategy is very cost effective and can be easily used. Forming a self-help group, for example, for women facing domestic violence can be easily started in a community. Any woman in the community can take the initiative to start such a group. Alternately, an organization can initiate the process by organizing a meeting or meetings in the community to raise awareness about the issue of domestic violence. The idea of starting a self-help group can be introduced in these meetings.

Pre-group meetings: In these meetings called pre group meetings, the concept of self-help group is explained to the women. The worker should explain the purpose of the group in some detail. Give concrete examples of what the group can do. The worker should encourage the women to discuss whatever doubts they may have and assure them that the decision to do whatever they want is entirely up to them. A beginning can be made by simply finding a place to meet and deciding a convenient time for holding the meetings. The issue of how frequently the group may meet should be left flexible. Even if in the beginning only a few women decide to join, this should not discourage the worker. The same pattern can be followed for women facing other problems, particularly in a poor community.

Parents having children with disabilities or having problems in schools, can be contacted through institutions and hospitals and introduced to the idea of self-help groups. Similarly wives of prisoners can also be helped to form self-help groups, getting the information from the prison authorities.

Once the groups get started, the worker will have to facilitate the members in conducting their meetings. The worker can give them some general guidelines such as:

- The number of members should not generally exceed 10
- Give each member an opportunity to speak
- Do not criticize a member in a negative manner
- Do not interrupt while a person is speaking
- Give your full attention to the person while s/he is speaking
- Learn to trust each other
- Share the strategies that helped you in coping with the problem
- Try to be precise in narration
- Avoid talking all the time
- Think about how each member can be of help to the group.

Identifying some members who can take over the leadership role and undertaking a programme of training them to conduct group meetings will help in sustaining the groups. The groups can also be provided with some helpline numbers to contact in case they run into any problems or if they have any issues, which they wish to discuss with the worker.

Self-Help Groups for Meeting Community Needs

Self-help groups can manage many social issues. When properly formed and linked to one another, they are able to provide a broad range of social benefits to members and even to entire villages. With limited external inputs, groups take on community-wide social problems such as dowry and alcohol abuse. Further, they can also attract resources to build roads, bring in electricity and supply credit from government and private institutions. These groups make ideal platforms for launching an emergency prevention programme. Women are confident, organized and have funds saved to invest in protective measures for the households. In isolation, an SHG cannot prevent a natural disaster from turning into an emergency for a community. In India, many villages contain at least 100 families, with some having many more. Five or six self-help groups can cover the entire village. To allow for village level planning, SHGs must bind themselves together into a coherent system of communication and decision-making. Women must not only work together but must also bring in all members of a community, not just those in SHGs. SHGs can be trained to mobilize villagers for tackling different issues. By using a participatory learning and action methodology, a network of SHGs can empower villagers. A recent study shows that:

> (1) families feel more confident in managing a potential crisis; (2) some families have considered changing animal raising practices and cropping patterns to avert flood impact; (3) communities have created infrastructure to prevent loss of life (e.g., raised platforms and school-based shelters); (4) families have established grain reserves in protected bins/silos and have sealed important documents in plastic bags; and (5) for the first time in these villages women have actively participated in Gram Sansad meetings (local governance structure) to effect important policy changes and secure government resources to construct roads, bridges and wells in their communities (see Wilson, 2002; Sarah, 2002).

Starting a self-help group for tackling community problems alone will pose far more difficulties in India. A self-help group to deal with community problems is difficult to stabilize unless persons in the community are really committed, which is rarely the case. People in the community are generally struggling with very difficult life situations and find it difficult to spare time and resources. It is therefore easier to widen the scope of the groups already formed for savings and credits or other purposes and link them together to provide a forum for tackling community problems. Some training inputs can help the groups to identify their problems and by using a participatory approach, create a priority to deal with problems like water, electricity, and roads, etc., as these are generally the felt community needs. The worker can facilitate groups which have already taken the first step of holding some informal meetings to discuss the common problems. The worker can help them to:

- Set goals or to identify problems and decide about their priority.
- Clarify the importance of community participation.
- Explain the process of discussing both the problems and the strategies to solve the problems with all concerned people in the community.

- Provide information about possible government departments which could be of help.
- Encourage them to be self-reliant and to generate indigenous resources to meet their problems.
- Develop trust among different sections in the community.
- Develop a system of rotating leadership and provide leadership training.
- Help them to review the work of the group.
- Help them to distribute responsibilities.
- Help them to maintain proper records of all financial transactions and all decisions taken by the group.
- Help them to learn to share all the information with the community.

If there are many groups that a worker is handling at a time, it may be more cost effective to organize capacity building programmes for potential leaders or all members showing interest and regularly attending the group meetings and shouldering specific responsibilities (see the chapter on Process of Working with Groups as well).

Some cases of formation of self-help groups in various countries are given below to provide information about different experiments done in the field of using self-help groups. This is not to suggest that self help groups in these countries are being used for these purposes alone. The uses which are similar to the ones described above, are not mentioned here. For example, the saving and credit groups of women and farmers are being formed in a number of countries, including Pakistan, Bangladesh and Sri Lanka.

Self-Help Groups in Bangladesh

The Bangladesh Solidarity Group System

A group of five members is formed with the understanding that each will follow the group norms. Later, the monitoring financial institution (MFI) will help them to join a 'Centre' of around five to seven such groups. The MFI checks that all members are poor and are not related. The members make regular savings with the MFI and also take regular loans. They each have individual savings and loan accounts with the MFI and the main function of the groups and the Centre is to facilitate the financial intermediation process through performing tasks such as:

- Holding regular and usually weekly centre level meetings supervised by an MFI worker who maintains the records, where savings and repayments are collected and handed over to the MFI worker.
- Organizing contributions to one or a number of group savings funds, which can be used by the group for a number of purposes, usually only with the agreement of the MFI, which maintains the group fund accounts.
- Guaranteeing loans to their individual members by accepting joint and several liability, by raising group emergency funds and by accepting that no members of a Group will be able to take a new loan if any members are in arrears.
- Appraising fellow-members' loan applications, and ensuring that their fellow-members maintain their regular savings contributions and loan repayments.

This effort at introducing a micro finance scheme to rural poor women earned The Noble Peace Prize for the year 2006 for Mohammed Yunus, the founder of the Grameen Bank in Bangladesh.

Participatory Rural Development in Pakistan Through Self-Help Groups

The Food and Agriculture Organization (FAO) in 1989 started a project with the help of the University of Faisalabad. The project aims at testing the self-help group approach to reach small farmers and the rural poor. The self-help groups (membership varies from 5-15 members per group) operate at the village level and each is organized around common income-generating activities identified by the group members. They are supported by specially-trained group promoters (GPs) who live in the action areas.

Groups

Small groups of people, both male and female, have been formed into groups to help them overcome their poverty. GPs have been trained with regard to group formation, group dynamics, leadership, and income generation activities. The groups do not meet by themselves on a regular basis. Instead, they meet at the GP's office, generally twice a month, to deposit their savings, which is then deposited by the GP in the bank. An entry is made in the Group Savings Book. The group leader usually accompanies the GP to the bank to obtain the loan once it is approved. When the groups meet at the office of the GP, they only discuss issues concerning the income generating activities (IGAs). However, some groups also discuss other issues such as anti-narcotic drive, health and sanitation and nutrition, etc. A group also arranged a cricket match once.

Female Groups

Women groups are weak, both in performance as well as in group activities. Lady group promoters (LGPs) find it difficult to form the groups. Even when the groups are formed, the meetings are irregular and the women do not come to the GP's office. However, their saving and loan repayment activities are routinely done.

Income-Generating Activities

The most common income generating activities are livestock development, cattle fattening, sale of milk, goat raising and sale of poultry meat. Some new activities under consideration are electric motor winding, small transformer fabrication, wood sawing, and ladies hairpin manufacture. Women are mostly engaged in poultry production, milk selling, stitching, etc. Individual group members allocate the activities among themselves and the profits are equally divided with no questions asked.

Savings and Loans

The Consolidated Progress Reports indicate a steady increase of savings and loan repayments. Three out of four action areas have all repaid the loans in full and the other 75 per cent of the loan has been repaid. The savings of the groups are generally not withdrawn and are reflected in their individual pass books. These entries are made by the GPs in the individual savings books as the members are illiterate.

The loans are recommended by the GP and the Mobile Credit Officers (MCOs) of the Agricultural Development Bank of Pakistan (ADBP) after careful scrutiny of the IGAs, loan requirement and the repayment capacity. The GPs and the MCOs carefully monitor the utilization of credit, production and marketing and ensure that the loan is repaid at the correct time. It must be stated that the success of the loan repayment is largely due to the desire of the members not to get indebted to the bank as well as to the supervisory credit disbursement by the GP/MCOs.

The saving and credit has come to stay in the project and has paved the way for the banking culture to be established in the rural economy where the members are poor, illiterate, and devoid of assets as collateral required to gain entry to the credit system of the banks.

Group Promoters (GPs)

The GPs are performing well in the project. Their training is regularly updated through refresher courses designed to keep them abreast of the latest technical and managerial aspects of their work. They live and work in the area full time.

Inter-Group Associations

Inter-group associations have not yet been formed. The main problem is the distance, as transport facilities are inefficient and expensive (Nilaweera, 1996).

Drug Prevention Among Youth in Pakistan Through the Use of SHGs

Establishment of SHGs of Young People in Peshawar

Self-help groups of young people are formed to enable them to use a peer to-peer approach for drug abuse prevention activities. The young people are chosen as the target group because they are more likely to experiment with and use drugs.

The project is based on the assumption that drug and development problems are closely related. Thus the work to reduce drug abuse is seen not only as controlling certain substances but also as reducing poverty, promoting development of women and youth, providing healthy alternatives to drug use and empowering people as agents of change.

Major activities include:

- Conducting a survey of living conditions among the youth of Peshawar to serve as a baseline for needs-driven prevention of drug abuse
- Holding training workshops for youth and teachers

- Initiating and supporting self-help groups
- Building networks

The overall goal of the project was to empower young people to communicate with their peers about the dangers of drug use and to conduct prevention activities among their peers that would reduce drug abuse and the risk of addiction.

It was difficult to ensure the sustainability of the self-help groups that had been established, especially without the support of the NGO.

Lessons learned

The peer-to-peer approach:

- Improves access to and contact with target groups that are normally difficult to reach;
- Increases acceptance of the prevention activities because young people themselves are responsible for planning and implementation;
- Facilitates the implementation of gender sensitive approaches;
- Helps young people, and their friends and families to realistically assess the risk of slipping into drug consumption and to take responsible decisions accordingly;
- Can be integrated into other health, social or educational development measures and readily adjusted to local conditions.
- Young people between 12 and 24 in Peshawar, especially from poorer social groups and especially young women, were identified and trained in drug prevention methods, as were the multipliers (teachers).
- The groups varied in size from 3-10 members, with seven members being the average.
- The aim of the self-help group was to reinforce the healthy behaviour of their peers through measures to prevent drug abuse and addiction.
- The activities carried out by the self-help groups included poster and essay competitions and making banners, holding fun fairs, drama performances and demonstrations, and creating materials such as badges and buttons with information about drugs and their effects.

- Socio-cultural and religious factors must be considered in the implementation of drug abuse prevention and intervention activities.
- Qualitative research prior to project design is essential for an understanding of socio-cultural and religious conditions (GTZ, 1999-2002).

Strengthening Small Farmer Groups in Sri Lanka

The Small Farmer Group Development Unit (SFGDU) of the Ministry of Agriculture, Lands and Forestry (MALF), in Sri Lanka promotes the development of small, self-reliant and sustainable groups and ensures their active participation in development. It develops or collects information on participatory development principles and practices and passes them to the rural development programmes. It also provide training in small group development methodologies to government officials involved in agricultural and rural development. The SFGDU has published several documents on small farmer group development and farmers organizations in Sinhala. These include posters, manuals on organization of small farmer groups and farmers' organization, women participation, case studies and reports of village studies and so on. It has published *The Group Promoters Resource Book* and The *Group Promoters Enterprise Book* which has also been translated into Sinhala. It is also publishing a monthly newsletter since January, 1996, which contains articles on small group formation and farmers organization, including case studies and views of small farmers.

The government has recruited about 20,000 Group Animators, who are assigned in the villages. Two persons are assigned in each village and one is assigned to work in agriculture. Training programmes are also organized, which range from one day orientation sessions for government officials, one day training for small farmer group (SFG) members, 2-3 days residential training for farmer leaders and 3-4 days residential training for Group Animators.

The management committee of the farmers organizations has been restructured so that all small farmers groups can be represented in the committee. Two representatives of each small farmers groups, will be nominated to the management committee at the Grama Dilahari divisional level. The officers of the farmers organizations will be rotated to give equal opportunity to represent the groups and be elected as officers (Reyes, 1996). The strategy is expected to make small farmers' groups more effective in rural development. The approach is similar to the one advocated by Kay (2002) to make the groups participation in developmental matters more comprehensive.

Bibliography

Abell, Mellssa L. and Maeda J. Galinsky (2002): "Introducing Students to Computer: Based Group Work Practice". *Journal of Social Work Education.* Vol. 38. No. 1. pp. 39-54.

Allison, G.T. (1971): *Essence of Decision: Explaining the Cuban Missile Crisis.* Boston: Little, Brown and Company.

Amster, F. (1943): "Differential Uses of Play in Treatment of Young Children". *American Journal of Orthopsychiatry.* 13, 62-68.

Arrow Holly, Marshall Scott Poole, Kelly B. Henry, Susan Wheelan and Richard Moreland (2004): "Time, Change and Development – The Temporal Perspective on Groups". *Small Group Research.* Vol. 35 (1). pp. 73-105.

Arrow, Holly, and Joseph, E. Mcgrath (1993): "Membership Matters – How Members Change and Continuity Affect Small Group Structure, Process and Performance". *Small Group Research.* Vol. 24 (3). pp. 334-361.

Bales, R. (1950): *Interaction Process Analysis: A Method for the Study of Small Groups.* Reading: Addison-Wesley Publishing Company.

Balgopal, P.R. and Vassil (1983): *Groups in Social Work: An Ecological Perspective.* New York: McMillan.

Bandhyopadya, P. (2002): "Convergence of Programmes by Empowering SHGs and PRIs". *Economic and Political Weekly.* 37(26), 2556-61.

Barbara, A.W., Kevin W. Moss Holder, Robert P. Steel, and Nathan Bennett (1998): "Does Work Group Cohesiveness Affect Individual's Performance and Organization Commitment". *Small Group Research.* Vol. 29 (4). pp. 472-497.

Bavelas, A. (1942): "Morale and the Training of Leaders" in G. Watson, (ed.) *Civilian Morale.* New York: Reynal & Hitchcock.

Bennis, Warren G., Kenneth Benne, and Robert Chin (eds.). (1961): *The Planning of Change*. New York: Holt, Rinehart & Winston, Inc., p. 698.

Berelson, Bernard and Gary A. Steiner (1964): *Human Behaviour*. New York: Harcourt Brace Jovanovich, Inc.

Berelson, Bernard and Gary A. Steiner (1964): *Human Behaviour: An Inventory of Scientific Findings*. New York: Harcourt, Brace and World.

Bernstein, Saul (1965): *Explorations in Group Work*. Boston: Boston University School of Social Work.

Bertcher, Harvey J. (1994): *Group Participation*. Thousand Oaks: Sage.

Berwald, Claudia and Tracy Houstra (2002): "Joining Feminism and Social Group Work Practice: A. Women's Disability Group". *Social Work with Groups*. Vol. 25 (4). pp. 71-83.

Bion's, W.R. (1961): *Experiences in Groups*. New York: Basic Books.

Blau, Peter M. (1964): *Exchange and Power in Social Life*. New York: John Wiley & Sons.

Breton, Margot (2002): "A Rewarding Group Workers Journey". *Social Work With Groups*. Vol. 25. No. 1-2. pp. 23-29.

Bright, Sallie (1955): "Letting the Public in on Group Work Objectives" in H.B. Trecker (ed.). *Group Work-Foundations and Frontiers*. New York: White Side Inc. and William Morrow and Co., pp. 35-49.

Brown, Allan (1997): "Group Work" in Martin Davies (ed.). *The Blackwell Companion to Social Work*. Oxford: Blackwell Publishers.

Brown, Allan and Clough Roger (1989) *Groups and Groupings*. London: Tavistock

Bunston, Wendy, Tara Pavlidis, and Paul Leyden (2003): "Putting the GRO in Group Work". *Australian Social Work*. Vol. 56. No. 1. pp. 40-49.

Butler, L. (1987): "Anatomy of Collusive Behaviour. NTL Connections, 4, 1 (1987)", 1-2. as quoted from *Groups Theory and Experience*. R.W. Napier and M.K. Greshenfeld, 2004. Boston: Houghton Mifflin.

Caplan, Tom and H. Thomas (2004): "The Effective Use of Common Themes in Diverse Group Selections". *Social Work With Groups*. Vol. 26(1). pp. 5-28.

Carll, E.K. (1994): "Disaster Intervention with Children and Families: National and State Initiatives". *The Child Youth and Family Services Quarterly.* 17, 21-23.

Cartwright, D. (1961): "Achieving Change in People" in Warren G. Bennis, Kenneth Benne, and Robert Chin, (eds.). *The Planning of Change*, New York: Holt, Rinehart & Winston, Inc., p. 698.

Cartwright, D. and Ronald Lippitt (1961): "Group Dynamics and the Individual" in Bennis, Benne, and Chin, (eds.) *The Planning of Change.* New York: Holt, Rinehart & Winston. Inc., p. 264.

Cartwright, D. and A. Zander (eds.) (1968): *Group Dynamics.* New York: Harper and Row.

Cattell, R.B. (1948): "Concepts and Methods in the Measurement of Group Syntality". *Psychological Review.* L.V., 48-63.

Cheshire, J.D. and Feroz, E.H. (1989): "Allison's Models and the FASB Statements Nos 2, 5, 13 and 19". *Journal of Business Finance and Accounting. 16 (1)* pp. 119-130.

Collins, Barry and Harold Guetzkow (1964): *A Social Psychology of Group Process for Decision Making.* New York: John Wiley & Sons, Inc.

Cooley, Charles H. (1909): *Social Organization.* New York: Charles Scribner's Sons.

Cooper, H.M. (1979): "Statistically Combing Independent Studies: A. Meta Analysis of Sex Differences in Conformity Research". *Journal of Personality and Social Psychology.* 37. pp. 131-146.

Corey, G. and Corey, M., (2006): *Groups: Process and Practice.* Belmont: Thomson.

Corey, Gerald (2000): *Theory and Practice of Group Counselling.* Brookes: Thomas Learning. pp. 38-47.

Coyle, Grace, L. (1930): *Social Process in Organized Groups.* New York: Richard R. Smith.

Coyle, Grace, L. (1948): *Group Work with American Youth: A Guide to the Practice of Leadership.* New York: Harper Brothers.

Coyle, Grace, L. (1947): "Group Work in Recreation". Proceedings of the National Conference of Social Work, New York: Columbia University Press.

Coyle, Grace, L. (1947): "On Becoming Professional" in AAGW (comp.), *Toward Professional Standards.* New York: Association Press, p. 18.

Coyle, Grace, L. (1947): *Group Experience and Democratic Values.* New York: Woman's Press, 1947. p. 95.

Coyle, Grace, L. (1947): "Group Work: A Method in Recreation". *The Group.* 9, April. pp. 8-11.

Deutsche Gesellschaft für Technische Zusammenarbeit (GTZ) (2002): Development-oriented Drug Control Programme (DDC): Germany. Eschborn.

Devasa, Leelamma and Antony Jancy (2004): "Social Development Issues in Self Help Groups". *Social Welfare.* 50(10), 4-9.

Douglas, Tom (1979): *Group Process in Social Work: A Theoretical Synthesis.* New York: Wiley.

Douglas, Tom (1983): *Groups.* London: Tavistock.

Durkin Helen E. (1967): *The Group in Depth.* New York: International Universities Press.

Dwivedi, K.N. (2005) (ed.): *Group Work with Children and Adolescents.* London: Jessica Kingsley Publishers.

Eagly, A.H. (1978): "Sex Differences in Influence-ability". *Psychological Bulletin.* 85. pp. 86-116.

Ekeh, Peter (1974): *Social Exchange Theory.* Cambridge: Harvard University Press.

Emerson, R.M. (1964): "Power Dependence Relations: Two Experiments". *Sociometery.* 1964. 27. 282-298.

Eubank, E.E. (1932): *Concepts of Sociology.* Boston: D.C. Heath and Co. p.163.

Feldman, R. (1986): "Group Work Knowledge and Research: A Two Decade Comparison". *Social Work With Groups.* Vol. 9 (3). pp. 7-14.

Fernandez, A.P. (1994): *The MYRADA Experience.* Bangalore: Myrada.

Festinger, Leon (1950): "Informal Social Communication". *Psychological Review.* Vol. 57. pp. 271-282.

Follett, Mary Parker (1934): *The New State.* New York: Longman.

Forte, J.A. (1994): "Around the World with Social Group Work: Knowledge and Research Contributions". *Social Work With Groups.* Vol. 17(1-2). pp. 143-162.

Freud, S. (1966): *Introductory Lectures on Psycho-analysis.* New York: Norton.

Garland, Jones and Kolondy (1976): "A Model of Stages of Group Development in Social Work Groups". In S. Bernstein (ed.). *Explorations in Group Work.* Boston: Charles River Books. pp. 17-71.

Garvin, Charles D., L.M. Guttirez and M.J. Galinsky (Edited) (2004): *Handbook of Group Work.* New York: Guilford Publication.

Gersick, C.J.G. (1988): "Time and Transition in Work Teams: Toward a New Model of Group Development". *Acad. Manage.* J. 31:41

Giddens A. (1989): *Sociology.* Cambridge: Polity Press. p. 275.

Glasser, P. and N. Mayadas (1986): *Group Workers a Work: Theory and Practice in the 80s.* Totowa, N.J.: Rowman and Littlefield.

Golembiewski, Robert (1962): *The Small Group.* Chicago: University of Chicago Press.

Goodman, Harriet and Manny Munoz (2004): "Developing Social Group Work Skills for Contemporary Agency Practice". *Social Work With Groups.* Vol. 27(1). pp. 17-33.

Government of India (1999): Swarnjyanti Gramin Swarozgar Yojna Guidelines, New Delhi: Ministry of Rural Development.

Greene, C.N. and Schriesheim, C.A. (1980): "Leader-group Interactions: A Longitudinal Field Investigation". *Journal of Applied Psychology.* 65:50-59

Grusec, J.E. and Lytton, Hugh (1988): *Social Development.* New York: Springer. p. 230.

GTZ (1999-2002): Drug Prevention Among Youth in Peshawar, Pakistan. http://w.w.w.2Gtz.de/dokumente/bib/D6-1056d.pdf.

Hare, Paul (1962): *Handbook of Small Group Research.* New York: Free Press.

Hartford, M.E. (1972): *Groups in Social Work.* New York: Columbia University Press.

Helanko, R. (1963): "Sports and Socialization" in Neil J. Smelser and William T. Smelser (eds.). *Personality and Social Systems.* New York: John Wiley & Sons, Inc.

Homans, G.C. (1950): *The Human Group.* New York: Harcourt Brace.

Homans, G.C. (1961): *Social Behaviour: Its Elementary Forms.* New York: Harcourt Brace.

Indira, Kumari Y. and Rao, Sambasiva B. (2001): "Emergence of Women Self Help Groups and its Impact on Rural Development: A Case Study in Krishna District in Andhra Pradesh". *Indian Journal of Agriculture Economics.* 56(3),483.

Jain, Devaki (1979): *In Search of Power.* New Delhi: Vikas.

Janis Andrews (2001): "Group Works Place in Social Work: A Historical Analysis". *Journal of Sociology and Social Welfare.* Vol. XXVIII. No. 4. pp. 45-65.

Janis, Irving L. (1982): *Groupthink: Psychological Study of Policy Decisions and Fiasco.* Boston: Houghton Mifflin.

Jeffery, Patricia (1979): *Frogs in a Well: Indian Women in Purdah.* New Delhi: Vikas.

Kaiser Clara A. (1959): "The Social Group Work Process" in Marjorie Murphy, (ed.). *The Social Group Work Method in Social Work Education.* Vol. XI. A Project Report on Curriculum Study. New York: Council on Social Work Education.

Katz, A.H. (1993): *Self Help in America: A Social Movement Perspective.* New York: Twayne.

Kay, Thelma (2002): "Empowering Women through Self-help Micro Credit Programmes". Bangkok: Gender and Development Section, ESCAP.

Kingman, J.M. and Sidman, S. (1935): 'Some Principles of Group Work' in A Manual of Settlement Boys' Work, National Federation of Settlements. Available in the informal education archives.

Kishwar, Madhu and Ruth Vanita (eds.) (1984): *In Search of Answers.* New Delhi: Horizon Books.

Kivisto, Peter (2003): *Social Theory: Roots and Branches,* Los Angeles: Roxbury Publishing Company.

Klein, Alan F. (1972): *Effective Group Work.* New York: Association Press.

Konopka, Gisela (1963): *Social Group Work: A Helping Process,* Englewood Cliffs, N.J.: Prentice-Hall. p. 8.

Kosof, Susan (2003): "Single Session Groups: Applications and Areas of Expertise". *Social Work With Groups.* Vol. 26(1). pp. 29-45.

Krishnaraj, Maithreyi and Thelma Kay (2002): Report of Review of IFAD Gender Mainstreaming Projects in Asia. Bangkok: Unpublished paper prepared for IFAD.

Kurland, Roselle, Robert Salmon, with Mary Bitel, Harriet-Goodman, Keren Ludwig, Emily W. Newmann and Nancy Sullivan (2004): "The Survival of Social Group Work: A Call to Action". *Social Work With Groups.* Vol. 27(1). pp. 3-16.

Lacoursiere, R.B. (1980): *The Life Cycle of Groups: Group Developmental Stage Theory.* New York: Human Science Press.

Lahiti, Ryan K. (1996): Group Decision Making within Organization: Can Models Help? Centre for Study Work Teams, University of North Texas.

Lang, N. (1981): "Some Defining Characteristics of the Social Work Group: Unique Social Form" in S., Abels and P. Abels (eds.). *Social Work with Groups,* Proceedings, First Symposium on Social Work with Groups, Hebron, Connecticut: Practitioners Press.

–. (2004): "Concurrent Interventions in Multiple Domains". *Essence of Social Work with Groups.* Vol. 27 (1). pp. 35-51.

Langfred, Claus W. (1998): "Is Group Cohesiveness a Double Edged Sword? An Investigation of the Effects of Cohesiveness on Performance". *Small Group Research.* Vol. 29 (2). pp. 124-143.

Leighton Alexander H. (1945): *The Governing of Men.* Princeton, N.J.: Princeton University Press.

Lesser, Joan G., N.R. O'Neill, K.W. Burke, P. Scanlon, K. Hollis and Rina Miller (2004): "Women Supporting Women: A Mutual Aid Group Fosters New Connections Among Women in Midlife". *Social Work With Groups.* Vol. 27 (1). pp. 75-88.

Levi-Strauss, Claud (1971): "The Principle of Reciprocity" in Lewis Coser and Bernard Rosenberg (eds.). *The Sociological Theory.* New York: Macmillan.

Levi-Strauss, Claude (1958): *Structural Anthropology.* London: Penguin.

Levine, M. John and Richard L Moreland (1990): "Progress in Small Group Research". *Annual Review of Psychology.* Vol. 41. pp. 585-634

Levine, Marion. S.: "Creating a Group Work Culture in a Children's (2002): Mental Health Agency: A Professional Memoir". *Social Work With Groups.* Vol. 25. No. 1-2. pp. 193-202.

Lewin, Kurt (1943): "Forces Behind Food Habits and Methods of Change". *National Research Council Bulletin.* CVIII.

Lewin, Kurt (1946): "Behaviour as a Function of the Total Situation" in L. Carmichael (ed.) *Manual of Child Psychology.* pp. 791-844. New York: John Wiley

Lewin, Kurt (1951): *Field Theory in Social Science.* New York: Harper & Row.

Lewis, Coser (1973): "Social Conflict and the Theory of Social Change" in Amitai Etzioni and Eva Etzioni (eds.) *Social Change.* New York: Basic Books.

Lippitt, Ronald, Jeanne Watson, and Bruce Westley (1958): *The Dynamics of Planned Change.* New York: Harcourt Brace Jovanovich, Inc.

Long, S. (1984): "Early Integration in Groups: A Group to Join and a Group to Create", *Human Relations.* Vol. 37. pp. 311-32.

Lyles, M.A. and Thomas, H. (1988): "Strategic Problem Formulation: Biases and Assumptions Embedded in Alternative Decision-Making Models". *Journal of Management Studies. 25 (2)* pp. 131-145.

Macgowan, Mark, J. (2003): "Increasing Engagement in Groups: Increasing Engagement in Groups". *Social Work With Groups.* Vol. 26 (1). pp. 5-28.

Mahler, C. (1969): *Group Counselling in the Schools.* Boston: Houghton Mifflin.

Malekoff, A. (2002): "The Power of Group Work with Kids: Lessons Learned". *Social Work With Groups.* Vol. 25(1-2). pp. 71-86.

Malinowski, B. (1944): *A Scientific Theory of Culture.* Oxford: Oxford University Press.

Manis, Melvin (1955): "Social Interaction and the Self Concept". *Journal of Abnormal and Social Psychology.* LI. 362-70.

Mannheim, Karl (1957): *Systematic Sociology.* (ed.) by J.S. Eros and W.A.C. Stewart, London: Routledge & Kegan Paul.

Mayadas, Nazneen, Rebecca Smith and Doreen Elliott (2004): "Social Group Work in a Global Perspective" in Charles D. Garvin et al. (Edited) *Handbook of Group Work.* New York: Guilford Publication.

McDavid, John W. and Herbert Harrari (1968): *Social Psychology.* New York: Harper & Row. p. 39.

Mead, G.H. (1934): *Mind, Self and Society.* Chicago: University of Chicago Press.

Meenai, Zubair (2003): *Empowering Rural Women: An Approach to Empowering Women Through Credit Based Self-Help Groups.* Delhi: Aakar Books.

Middleman, R. (1981): "The Use of Programme" in S. Abels and P. Abels: *Social Work With Groups.* (Proceedings of the 1979, Symposium). Louisville: Committee For the Advancement of Social Work with Groups. pp. 187-205.

Mills, Theodore (1967): *The Sociology of Small Groups.* Englewood Cliffs, N.J., Prentice Hall.

Monappa, Arun and Mirza Saiyadain (1994): *Personnel Management.* New Delhi: Tata McGraw Hill.

Moreland, R.L., and Levine, J.M. (1988): "Group Dynamics Over Time: Development and Socialization in Small Groups" in McGrath, J.E., (ed.) 1988. *The Social Psychology of Time: New Perspectives.* Newbury Park: Sage

Murphy, Marjorie (1959): *Social Group Work Method in Social Work Education.* New York: Council on Social Work Education.

Nanda, Y.C. (1995): Significance of Establishing Linkages with Self Help Groups and Banks. Mumbai: NABARD.

Napier, Rodney W. and Matti K. Gershenfeld (2004): *Groups Theory and Experience.* Boston: Houghton Miffin.

Newcomb, T. (1943): *Personality and Social Change.* New York: Dryden.

Nilaweera, Dixon (1996): Status report on participatory rural development in Pakistan's Punjab: New directions. Rome: FAO.

Northen, Helen and Roselle, Kurland (2001): *Social Work With Groups.* New York: Columbia University Press.

Northen Helen (1969): *Social Work With Groups.* New York: Columbia University Press.

Nosko, Anna (2002): "Adventures in Co-Leadership in Social Group Work Practice". *Social Work With Groups.* Vol. 25. No. 1-2. pp. 175-183.

O'Hanlon, W. and Weiner-Davies, M. (2003): *In Search of Solutions: A New Direction in Psychotherapy.* New York: Norton.

Orville, Brim, and Stanton Wheeler (1966): *Socialization after Childhood.* New York: John Wiley & Sons, Inc.

Perlman, Helen Harris (1957): *Social Case Work.* Chicago: University of Chicago Press

Pernell, Ruby (1962): Identifying and Teaching the Skill Component of Social Group Work. Paper presented at the annual meeting of the Council on Social Work Education. St. Louis. Mimeographed Graduate School of Social Work. University of Pittsburgh. No. 4366.

Phillips, Helen U. (1997): *Essentials of Social Group Work Skill.* New York: Association Press.

Polio, David. E. (2002): "The Evidence Based Group Work". *Social Work With Groups.* Vol. 25(4). pp 57-70.

Reyes, Basilio de los (1996): Progress in strengthening small farmer group development in Sri Lanka: Report of a review mission. FAO

Ridgeway, Cecilia, L. (1983): *The Dynamics of Small Groups.* New York: St. Martin's Press.

Robins, Stephen P. (1997): *Essentials of Organizational Behaviour.* New Jersey: Prentice Hall.

Ryland, Gladys (1958) *Employment Responsibilities of Social Group Work Graduates.* New York: Council on Social Work Education, p. 4.

Saino, Maria (2003): "A New Language for Groups: Multilingual and Multiethnic Group Work". *Social Work With Groups.* Vol. 256(1). pp. 69-82.

Saloshin, Etta Henriette (1954): Development of an Instrument for the Analysis of the Social Group Work. PhD Thesis (Unpublished): University of Minnesota, Minneapolis.

Sarah, Smith (2002): "Community Preparedness in Action". In Kim Wilson (Ed) The Role of Self Help Group Bank Linkage Programme in Preventing Rural Emergencies in India. Paper presented at the Seminar on SHG-bank Linkage Programme at New Delhi. Sponsored by NABARD.

Saulnier, C.F. (2003): "Goal Setting Process: Supporting Choice in a Feminist Group for Women with Alcohol Problems". *Social Work With Groups.* Vol. 26(1). pp. 47-68.

Schein, Edgar and Warren Bennis (1965): *Personal and Organizational Change Through Group Method.* New York: John Wiley & Sons, Inc.

Schneider, J.K., Shawver, M.M. and Martin, A. (1993): Applying a Political Model to Program Development. Nursing Management, 24 (10) pp. 52-55.

Schutz, Alfred (1962): *The Problem of Social Reality.* Vol. I. The Hague: Mijhoff.

Schutz, William C. (1958): *F.I.R.L.: A Three-Dimensional Theory of Interpersonal Orientation.* New York: Holt, Rinehart & Winston, Inc.

Sears, Pauline S. and V.S. Sherman (1964): *In Pursuit of Self-Esteem* Belmont, Calif., Wadsworth Publishing Co. Inc.

Sharry, John (2001): *Solution Focused Group Work.* London: Sage.

Shelby, J. (1994): "Psychological Intervention with Children in Disaster Relief Shelters". *The Child Youth and Family Services Quarterly. 17, 14-18.*

Sherif M. (1936): *The Psychology of Social Norms.* New York: Harper and Row.

Siddiqui, H.Y. (1987): "Towards a Competency Based Education". *Indian Journal of Social Work.* XLVIII, 1, 1987.

Siddiqui, H.Y. (1997): *Working With Communities.* New Delhi: Hira Publications.

Skidmore, Rex A. et al. (1988): *Introduction to Social Work.* Englewood Cliff: Prentice Hall.

Slavson, S.R. (1945, 1979): "Differential Methods in Relation to Age Levels" in M. Schiffer (ed.). *Dynamics of Group Psychotherapy.* New York: Jason Aronson.

Slavson, S.R. (1943): *Introduction to Group Therapy.* New York: Commonwealth Fund.

Solomon, Asch (1955): "Opinions and Social Pressure". *Scientific American.* Vol. CXCIII. pp. 31-35.

Srivastava, Alka (2004): *Self-Help Groups and Civil Society.* New Delhi: Indian Social Institute.

Sulman, Joanne, D. Savage Paul Vrooman and M. McGillivray (2004): "Social Group Work: Building a Professional Collective of Hospital Social Workers". *Social Work In Health Care.* Vol. 39(3-4). pp. 287-307.

Talcott, Parsons (1951): *Social Systems.* New York: The Free Press.

Terry, Robert (2001): *Seven Zones for Leadership.* Palo Alto, CA: Davies Black.

Thelen, Herbert (1954): *Dynamics of Groups at Work.* Chicago: University of Chicago Press, Phoenix Books.

Thomson, Janet and Ros Thorpe (2004): "Powerful Partnerships in Social Work: Group". *Australian Journal of Social Work.* Vol. 57. No. 1. pp. 46-56.

Tonnies, F. (1955): *Community and Association.* (Translated by C.P. Loomis). London.

Toseland, R.W. and Rivas R F (2001): *An Introduction to Group Work Practice.* Boston: Allyn and Bacon.

Trecker, H. (1980): "Administration as a Group Process: Philosophy and Concepts" in A Alissi (ed). *Perspectives on Social Group Work Practice.* pp. 332-337 New York: The Free Press.

Trecker, Harleigh B. (1948): *Social Group Work: Principles and Practices.* New York: Woman's Press.

Truman, David B. (1951): *The Governmental Process.* New York: Alfred A. Knopf, Incl.

Tuckman, B. and Jensen, M. (1977): *Stages of Small Group Development. Group and Organizational Studies.* 2, pp. 419-427.

Tuckman, B. (1963): "Developmental Sequence in Small Groups". *Psychological Bulletin.* 63, 384-399.

United Nations Development Programme (1997): Sustaining Livelihoods: Promoting Informal Sector Growth in Pacific Island Countries. Unpublished paper.

United Nations, (2001): Empowerment of Women Throughout the Life Cycle as a Transformative Strategy for Poverty Eradication. REPORT.

Vecchio, Robert P., R. Craig Bullis and Dona M. Brazil (2006): "The Utility of Situational Leadership Theory: A Replication in a Military Setting". *Small Group Research.* Vol. 37(5). pp. 407-424.

Whitaker, Dorothy Stock (1995): *Using Groups to Help People.* London: Routledge.

Wilson, Kim (2002): The Role of Self Help Group Bank Linkage Programme in Preventing Rural Emergencies in India. Paper presented at the Seminar on SHG-bank Linkage Programme at New Delhi. Sponsored by NABARD.

Wilson, Gertrude (1942): "Human Needs Pertinent to Group Work Services". Proceedings of the National Conference of Social Work, New York: Columbia University Press.

Wilson, Gertrude (1947): "Trends in Professional Education in Group Work" in AAGW (comp.), *Toward Professional Standards.* New York: Association Press. p. 33.

Wilson, Gertrude and Gladys Ryland (1949): *Social Group Work Practice.* Boston: Houghton Mifflin Co.

Wituk, Scott A. Shelly Tiemeyer, Amy Commer, Marry Warren, and Greg Meissen (2003): "Starting Self Help Groups: Empowering Roles for Social Workers". *Social Work With Groups.* Vol. 26 (1). pp. 83-92.

Wright, Whitney (2002): "But I Want to Do a Real Group". *Social Work With Groups.* Vol. 25. No. 1-2. pp. 107-112.

Yalom, I.D. (1995): *The Theory and Practice of Group Psychotherapy.* New York: Basic Books.

Zastrow, Charles and Karen K. Kirst-Ashman (1990): *Understanding Human Behaviour and the Social Environment.* Chicago: Nelson, Hall Publishers.

Index